ELEMENTARY TURKISH

by
LEWIS V. THOMAS

Late Professor of Oriental Studies
Princeton University

Revised and Edited by
NORMAN ITZKOWITZ

Professor of Near Eastern Studies
Princeton University

DOVER PUBLICATIONS, INC.
NEW YORK

For P. K. H. and M. G. H.

This Dover edition, first published in 1986, is an unabridged and slightly corrected republication of the work originally published by Harvard University Press, Cambridge, Massachusetts, in 1967.

Manufactured in the United States of America
Dover Publications, Inc., 31 East 2nd Street, Mineola, N.Y. 11501

Library of Congress Cataloging in Publication Data

Thomas, Lewis V. (Lewis Victor), 1914–1965.
  Elementary Turkish.

  Reprint. Originally published: Cambridge, Mass. : Harvard University Press, 1967.
  1. Turkish language—Conversation and phrase books—English.
I. Itzkowitz, Norman. II. Title.
PL127.T4 1986   494'.3582421   85-29194
ISBN 0-486-25064-4

Editor's Note

LEWIS VICTOR THOMAS was born in Chicago, February 27, 1914, and died in Princeton, October 21, 1965. He grew up in Indiana and was proud of his Hoosier background. He was trained as a classicist and orientalist at the University of Chicago and its Oriental Institute. Shortly after World War II he took his Ph.D. under Paul Wittek at Brussels. In 1947 he joined the Princeton faculty.

An accomplished teacher, Thomas made his seminars in Ottoman history and his courses in the Turkish language a training ground for many of America's growing group of Ottomanists and Turkish specialists. As a teacher he was keenly aware of the lack of adequate teaching materials. During his last year Thomas was hard at work preparing this grammar for publication, but his illness prevented him from completing the project to which he had devoted so much effort. He asked me to see the book through to publication, and I have made the necessary revisions with the kind assistance of Mr. Salih Necdet Ok, whose help I gratefully acknowledge.

In the process of editing the manuscript I have preserved almost all of Thomas's organization and method. This book has helped many Princeton students to learn modern Turkish quickly. It is hoped that it will now enable even more students to achieve that goal and that through them Lewis V. Thomas's influence will continue in the field of Turkish studies that he served so well.

Norman Itzkowitz

Preface

THE PURPOSE of this book is to enable English-speaking students to recognize, understand, and begin to use the basic patterns of modern standard Turkish. These basic patterns are, insofar as possible, presented one by one in a sequence that experience has shown to yield maximum results for English speakers.

The exercises are intended to present the student with the elements of Turkish in a form which he can begin to use. New vocabulary occurring in the exercises can be located in the Glossary.

An effort has been made to limit the material presented to those forms and patterns that in fact make up elementary standard modern Turkish. My thanks are due to the generations of Princeton University students who have uncomplainingly used the book in its successive mimeographed editions and in so doing have helped me learn what elementary Turkish is. Thanks are also due to my colleagues Professor Norman Itzkowitz and Mr. Cevat Erder and to a valiant typist, Mrs. Elsa Washington.

Lewis V. Thomas

Contents

1

2

Lesson 1

The Alphabet. 'Soft g.' Doubled Consonants.

The Circumflex Accent. Spelling.

Syllabification. Punctuation

---

1. The alphabet

The Turkish alphabet contains 29 letters. *Q, w,* and *x* do not occur. Six Turkish letters are unfamiliar to the American student's eye. They are the three consonants *ç, ğ,* and *ş,* and the three vowels *ı, ö,* and *ü.* The capital forms of these letters are *ç, Ç, ğ, Ğ, ş, Ş, ı, I, ö, Ö,* and *ü, Ü.* Note that the capital form of *ı* (called the 'undotted i') is *I;* that of *i* (the 'dotted i') is *İ.*

LETTER		NAME	APPROXIMATE PRONUNCIATION
A	a	a	as *u* in *sun*
B	b	be	as in English
C	c	ce	as *j* in *jump*
Ç	ç	çe	as *ch* in *church*
D	d	de	as in English
E	e	e	as in *fed*
F	f	fe	as in English
G	g	ge	as in *go*

3

LETTER		NAME	APPROXIMATE PRONUNCIATION
Ğ	ğ	yumuşak ge (soft g)	as *y* in *yet* (See the note in Lesson 1, section 2.)
H	h	he	as in *head*
I	ı	ı	as the second vowel in *nation*
İ	i	i	as in *bit*
J	j	je	as *s* in *measure*
K	k	ke	as in *king*
L	l	le	as in English
M	m	me	as in English
N	n	ne	as in English
O	o	o	as *o* in *falsetto*
Ö	ö	ö	as *eu* in French *peu*
P	p	pe	as in English
R	r	re	as in *rock*
S	s	se	as in *sit*
Ş	ş	şe	as *sh* in *shoe*
T	t	te	as in English
U	u	u	as *u* in *pull*
Ü	ü	ü	as *ü* in *über*
V	v	ve	as in English
Y	y	ye	as in *yellow*
Z	z	ze	as in English

In general, stress tends to be placed on the last syllable in a word.

2. 'Soft g'

Ğ, ğ (*yumuşak ge* 'soft g'). This letter never begins a word. When it immediately follows a back vowel, a vowel formed in the back of the mouth (*a, ı, o, u*: see Lesson 4, section 4), its sound resembles the glide one hears between the words 'go on' or between the words 'go over' when either of these pairs of words is slurred (as in *ağaç* 'tree'). When *yumuşak ge* immediately follows a front vowel, a vowel formed in the front of the mouth (*e, i, ö, ü*: see Lesson 4), its sound is approximately that of *y* in 'yet' (as in *diğer* 'other').

3. Doubled consonants

The sound of a doubled consonant is prolonged well beyond that of the same consonant when single.

elli   fifty   **eli**   the hand (objective)

4

4. The circumflex accent

The circumflex accent (^) may stand over the vowels *a*, *i*, and *u* (*â*, *î*, *û*). It has two distinct functions.

a. Standing over the letter *a* which is preceded by *g*, *k*, or *l* (*gâ*, *kâ*, *lâ*), the circumflex indicates that a *y* sound is to be pronounced between the consonant and the following *a*. In the syllable *lâ*, the *y* sound is fainter than in the syllables *gâ* and *kâ*.

gâvur	heathen
kâr	profit (compare *kar* 'snow')
lâle	tulip

b. Except in the syllables *gâ*, *kâ*, and *lâ*, the circumflex indicates that the vowel sound is to be prolonged. This is the case in the many (originally Arabic) adjectives ending in *î*.

Şamî	Damascene (*Şam* 'Damascus')
Lübnanî	Lebanese (*Lübnan* 'the Lebanon')
millî	national
edebî	literary
iktisadî	economic, economical

Sometimes the circumflex is used to distinguish between two words which, without it, would be spelled and pronounced identically.

Ali   proper name (of a man)   **âli**   lofty, sublime

Occasionally a word beginning with *ga*, *ka*, or *la* has a long vowel in the first syllable but does not have in that syllable the *y* sound which the use of a circumflex (*gâ*, *kâ*, *lâ*) would indicate. This may be shown by doubling the *a*, e.g. *kaatil* 'murderer.' Compare *katil* 'murder.'

5. Spelling

Turkish spelling is phonetic, the same letter always indicating the same sound. Words borrowed from other languages are frequently spelled out phonetically.

Şevrole   Chevrolet   *Çörçil*   Churchill

NOTE: Any sequence of vowel immediately followed by vowel is to be pronounced with a full stop between the two vowels. (The use of *aa* to indicate

5

long *a* in a word like *kaatil* 'murderer' [see above, section 4b] is the sole exception to this rule.) Words containing the sequence vowel–vowel are always of non-Turkish origin. Some Turkish writers and presses use an apostrophe to show the full stop between the two vowels, but this is now very rare. The stop is always to be made, whether an apostrophe is used or not.

saat or sa'at	hour, time: watch, clock
Sait or Sa'it	proper name (of a man)

(For other uses of the apostrophe, see Lesson 4.)

6. Syllabification

Turkish admits six syllable patterns (V = vowel; C = consonant).

V	*o*	he, she, it; that (demonstrative)
VC	*ak*	white
CV	*ve*	and
CVC	*dağ*	mountain
VCC	*üst*	top
CVCC	*genç*	young

Each syllable begins with a single vowel or with a single consonant. Borrowed words which begin with two consonants may undergo one of two changes.

a. A vowel is inserted between the two initial consonants

     kıral   king

b. A vowel is prefixed to the first consonant.

     ispirto   spirits, alcohol

c. With some borrowings, however, this does not occur.

     kredi   credit

7. Punctuation

Turkey's authors, editors, and publishers have not yet standardized punctuation. The period and question mark are ordinarily used as they are in English. A comma often indicates the end of the subject. Direct quotations may be shown by single or double quotation marks, by continental quotation marks, by dashes, or even by parentheses. Frequently, only the beginning of a quotation is shown. Often, a quotation is not indicated at all.

Exercises

A. Practice aloud.

anne	mother	dört beş	four (or) five
baba	father	dört beş	four (or) five
altı	six	çocuk	children
kaç?	how much?	ev	house
	how many?	erken	early
altı ağaç	six trees	fena	bad
kaç ağaç?	how many trees?	fincan	cup
bir	one; a, an	fil	elephant
beş	five	hafta	week
ben	I	kaç hafta?	how many weeks?
büyük	big, large, great	bir fincan	one cup; a cup
balık	fish	büyük cami	big mosque
beş balık	five fish	fena fil	bad elephant
cadde	street, avenue	gün	day
cami	mosque	göl	lake
sözcü	spokesman	geniş	wide
gece	night	göz	eye
kaç gece?	how many nights?	fena gün	bad day
beş cadde	five streets	büyük göl	big lake
bir gece	one night; a night	oğul	son
		yağ	grease, (cooking) fat, (vegetable) oil
çocuk	child (male or female)		
büyük çocuk	big child, boy	çok yağ	lots of grease
çok	much, many, very	diğer	(the) other
		diğer göz	(the) other eye
çok büyük	very big	eğer	if
çok gece	many nights	eğer ben	if I . . .
güç	difficult	bahçe	garden, yard
geç	late	sabah	morning
dört	four	kahve	coffee, coffeehouse
dokuz	nine	kaşık	spoon
doksan	ninety	şeker	sugar
diş	tooth	bir fincan kahve	one cup of coffee, a cup of coffee
dokuz diş	nine teeth		
doksan gece	ninety nights	kaç kaşık şeker?	how many spoons of sugar?
çok cami	many mosques		

7

dokuz kaşık	nine spoons	meyva	fruit
iki	two	çok meyva	much fruit,
iyi	good		lots of fruit
iyi gün	good day	et	meat
fena gün	bad day	ekmek	bread
biz	we	çok ekmek	much bread
siz	you (polite	bir ekmek	one (a) bread
	singular,		(i.e., a loaf of
	normal plural)		bread)
altmış	sixty	sen	you (familiar
hayır	no (opposite of		singular)
	'yes')	onlar	they
kırk	forty	limon	lemon
kısa	short	çok limon	lots of lemons,
Japonya	Japan		lots of lemon
garaj	garage	on	ten
kız	girl, daughter,	on bir	eleven
	maiden, female	on iki	twelve
kim?	who?	on beş hafta	fifteen weeks
küçük	small, little	o	he, she, it; that
küçük kız	little girl		(demonstrative),
el	hand		those
elli	fifty	o ev	that house
lira	lira (pound: unit	o beş ev	those five houses
	of money; the	kolay	easy
	Turkish Lira	dört göz	four eyes
	contains 100	dört büyük göz	four big eyes
	kuruş)	pul	stamp
kuruş	kuruş		(postage, etc.)
	(unit of money)	peynir	cheese
kaç lira?	how many liras?	kaç pul?	how many
kaç kuruş?	how many kuruş?		stamps?
	how much	parça	piece
	(does x cost)?	top	ball, sphere
40 lira	forty Turkish	renk	color
40 kuruş	Liras and	bardak	drinking glass
	forty kuruş	su	water
kol	arm	bir bardak su	a glass of water
akşam	evening	beş bardak su	five glasses of
minare	minaret		water

8

şey	thing	yüz	face; hundred
şey...	uh-uh ahem...(said when one hesitates in speech)	ve	and
		siz ve biz	you and we
		evet	yes
şimdi	now	havuz	pool
baş	head	gâvur	heathen
at	horse	yüksek	tall, high
otuz	thirty	yıl	year
otuz dokuz at	thirty-nine horses	yeni	new
süt	milk	ayak	foot
sütçü	milkman	az	few, (a) little,
Türk	Turk, Turkish		insufficient
bu	this, these	sekiz	eight
bu ev	this house	seksen	eighty
bu üç ev	these three houses	kâr	profit
şu	that (demonstrative), those (far over yonder)	kar	snow
		lâle	tulip
		Şam	Damascus
		Şamî	Damascene
şu ev	that house	Ali	man's name
şu beş ev	those five houses	âli	lofty, sublime

B. Practice the following words aloud.

1. COUNTING

bir	one	yirmi	twenty
iki	two	otuz	thirty
üç	three	kırk	forty
dört	four	elli	fifty
beş	five	altmış	sixty
altı	six	yetmiş	seventy
yedi	seven	seksen	eighty
sekiz	eight	doksan	ninety
dokuz	nine	yüz	(one) hundred
on	ten		

2. PRONOUNS

ben	I	biz	we
sen	you (familiar singular)	siz	you (plural, polite singular)
o	he, she, it	onlar	they

9

3. DEMONSTRATIVES

bu	this, these	**şu**	that, those (at a considerable distance,
o	that, those		see Lesson 7, section 3)

4. INTERROGATIVES

kim?	who?	**ne zaman?**	when? (what time?)
ne?	what?	**kaç?**	how much? how many?

5. PROPER NAMES

of men		of women	
Ahmet	**Ali**	**Suat**	**Fahrünnisa**
Mehmet	**Erdoğan**	**Süheylâ**	**Selma**
Sait		**Mihri**	

NOTE 1: Mehmet is the Turkish form of the Arabic name Muḥammad. The full form (Muhammed) is used in Turkish only to indicate the prophet of Islam.

NOTE 2: In modern usage, *Bay*, placed before a man's full name, represents English 'Mr.'

Bay Mehmet Timuroğlu Mr. Mehmet Timuroğlu

For the names of women, *Bayan* indicates either 'Mrs.' or 'Miss.'

Bayan Selma Timuroğlu Mrs. Selma Timuroğlu (or)
Miss Selma Timuroğlu

In addition to this modern and official usage, there remains in everyday currency an older usage, dating from the time when Turks had not yet adopted last names. In this style of address, the word *Bey* placed after a man's given name represents English 'Mr.'

Mehmet Bey   (Mr.) Mehmet

İsmail Hakkı Bey   (Mr.) İsmail Hakkı (İsmail Hakkı is a double given name, not a first and last name in the Western sense. Today this man might also appear as Bay İ. H. Ağaoğlu.)

In the older usage the word *Hanım* placed after the given name (or names) represents English 'Mrs.' or 'Miss.'

Mihri Hanım Mrs. Mihri (or) Miss Mihri

Persons who continue to use the older forms regard them as being no less formal than the new forms.

6. MODIFIERS

büyük	big, large, great	**kolay**	easy
küçük	little, small	**geç**	late
güç	difficult	**erken**	early

iyi	good, well	çok	much, many; very
fena	bad, badly	az	few, (a) little, insufficient

7. TIME

yıl	year	akşam	evening
ay	month	saat	hour, time;
hafta	week		watch, clock
gün	day	dakika	minute
gece	night	saniye	second
sabah	morning		

8. FAMILY

anne	mother	oğul	son
baba	father	kız	daughter, maiden,
çocuk	child		girl, female

9. THE BODY

baş	head	diş	tooth
yüz	face	kol	arm
göz	eye	el	hand
kulak	ear	bacak	leg
ağız	mouth	ayak	foot

10. THE CITY

şehir	city	ev	house
kasaba	town	bahçe	garden
köy	village	cami	mosque
cadde	avenue, street	minare	minaret

11. EATING

çay	tea	limon	lemon
kahve	coffee, coffeehouse	elma	apple
su	water	portakal	orange
süt	milk	ekmek	bread
bardak	drinking glass		(loaf of) bread
fincan	cup	peynir	cheese
yağ	grease, fat, oil	şeker	sugar, candy
meyva	fruit	tereyağ	butter

11

C. Practice saying the names of these Turkish cities and geographical features. Write them, dividing them into syllables.

1. CITIES

Adana		**İstanbul**
Afyonkarahisar		**Kars**
afyon	poppy, opium	**Kayseri**
kara	black	**Konya**
hisar	fortress	**Kütahya**
Balıkesir		**Malatya**
Bursa		**Samsun**
Diyarbekir		**Trabzon**
Edirne		**Yenişehir**
Erzurum		*yeni* new
Eskişehir		
eski	old	
şehir	city	

2. GEOGRAPHICAL FEATURES

Akdeniz	Mediterranean Sea	**Marmara Denizi**	Sea of Marmara
ak	white	**Van Gölü**	Lake (of) Van
deniz	sea	**Ağrı Dağı**	Mt. Ararat (Mountain of Ağrı)
Boğaziçi	Bosporus		
Çanakkale		**Allahüekber**	the Allahüekber Mountains
Boğazı	Dardanelles	**Dağları**	
Ege Denizi	Aegean Sea	*Allahü ekber*	God is greatest (Arabic)
İskenderun	Gulf of		
Körfezi	Iskenderun	**Erciyaş Dağı**	Mt. Argaeus
İzmir Körfezi	Gulf of Izmir	**Kavaşşahap**	the Kavushshap Mountains
Karadeniz	Black Sea	**Dağları**	
Tuz Gölü	Salt Lake	**Toros Dağları**	the Taurus Mountains
Kızılırmak	Red River		
kızıl	red, scarlet		
ırmak	river, stream		

Lesson 2

Cardinal Numbers. 'One Half.'

Kaç, Çok, and *Az. Parça* and *Tane*

1. Cardinal numbers

bir ev	one house, a house
bir kere	one time, one occurrence, once
bir defa	one time, one occurrence, once
iki ev	two houses, the two houses

NOTE: Turkish has no separate word for 'the' (the definite article). Hence every 'absolute' noun (i.e., the simple noun form with no suffix attached) may mean 'X' or 'the X.'

ev	house (or) the house	*peynir*	cheese (or) the cheese
üç çocuk	(the) three children	sekiz hafta	(the) eight weeks
dört cami	(the) four mosques	dokuz fincan	(the) nine cups
beş cadde	(the) five streets	on kız	(the) ten girls
altı gece	(the) six nights	bin bir gece	(the) thousand and
yedi gün	(the) seven days		one nights

Cardinal numbers are followed by singular nouns.

The cardinal numbers are:

bir	1	sekiz	8	on beş	15
iki	2	dokuz	9	on altı	16
üç	3	on	10	on yedi	17
dört	4	on bir	11	on sekiz	18
beş	5	on iki	12	on dokuz	19
altı	6	on üç	13	yirmi	20
yedi	7	on dört	14	yirmi bir	21

13

yirmi iki	22	otuz bir	31	doksan	90
yirmi üç	23	otuz iki	32	yüz	100
yirmi dört	24	otuz üç	33	yüz bir	101
yirmi beş	25	(etc.)	(etc.)	yüz iki	102
yirmi altı	26	kırk	40	yüz on	110
yirmi yedi	27	elli	50	yüz on bir	111
yirmi sekiz	28	altmış	60	iki yüz	200
yirmi dokuz	29	yetmiş	70	dokuz yüz	
otuz	30	seksen	80	doksan dokuz	999

bin	1,000	yüz bin	100,000
bin bir	1,001	(bir) milyon	1,000,000
on bin	10,000	(bir) milyar	1,000,000,000

2. 'One half'

There are two common words for 'one half.'

yarım, used when no other number is mentioned in the expression

yarım kilo	$\frac{1}{2}$ kilogram
beş yüz gram	500 grams
yarım kilometre	$\frac{1}{2}$ kilometer
beş yüz metre	500 meters
yarım saat	$\frac{1}{2}$ hour
otuz dakika	30 minutes

buçuk, used with numerals

bir buçuk saat	$1\frac{1}{2}$ hours
on buçuk kilometre	$10\frac{1}{2}$ kilometers
iki buçuk kilo	$2\frac{1}{2}$ kilos

3. Kaç, çok, and az

Like the cardinal numbers, the 'counting words' kaç 'how much?' 'how many?' çok 'much,' 'many,' and az 'few, 'a little' are followed by singular nouns.

kaç lira?	how many liras?	kaç dolar?	how many dollars?
kaç kuruş?	how many kuruş?	kaç kaşık	how many spoons
kaç para?	how much money?	şeker?	of sugar?

14

kaç elma?	how many apples?	az ev	few houses
çok ev	many houses, lots of houses	az para	little money, not much money
çok şeker	much sugar, lots of sugar	çok az para	very little money
		biraz şeker	a little sugar
çok limon	many lemons, lots of lemons, lots of lemon	birçok gazete	a good many newspapers
		az çok	more or less

4. Parça and tane

These two 'counting words' are to be distinguished from each other:

parça 'piece' (one part, section, segment, etc., of a whole);

tane 'piece' (the meaningless pidgin English counting word 'piece' as in 'one piece man,' 'one piece house,' i.e., 'one man,' 'one house') *Tane* may be used or omitted after the cardinal numbers.

kaç parça ekmek?	how many pieces of bread? (For 'slice' use *dilim*.)
kaç tane ekmek?	how many 'breads?' how many loaves of bread?
kaç ev?	how many houses?
kaç tane ev?	how many houses?
beş ev	five houses
beş tane ev	five houses
beş tane	five (of whatever is being counted)

Exercises

A. Count aloud to 100, from 100 to 200 by 5's, from 200 to 300 by 10's, from 300 to 500 by 20's.

B. Practice aloud. Translate.

1. Kaç kilo et?
2. ½ kilo kahve
3. az su
4. 1½ kilo şeker
5. birkaç kere
6. birkaç kilo elma
7. 250 gram tereyağ
8. 5 fincan çay
9. çok az limon
10. 12 tane portakal
11. 3½ saat
12. 30 cadde
13. 2½ lira
14. Kaç tane elma?
15. Kaç kuruş?
16. 3½ elma

17. 60 saniye	34. çok elma
18. 60 dakika	35. 1 baş
19. 24 saat	36. 2 el
20. 1 gün	37. 2 ayak
21. 7 gün	38. 2 göz
22. 4 hafta	39. çok az limon
23. 12 ay	40. 2 bardak su
24. 365 gün	41. az su
25. 100 yıl	42. biraz süt
26. 2 ağaç	43. çok az süt
27. 3 oğul	44. 10,000 kilometre
28. Kaç kilo şeker?	45. 8 gazete
29. $\frac{1}{2}$ kilo şeker	46. $\frac{1}{2}$ bardak su
30. 100 defa	47. $7\frac{1}{2}$ saat
31. Kaç para?	48. 2 dilim ekmek
32. az para	49. 3 kaşık şeker
33. Kaç tane limon?	50. 3 tane ekmek

C. Write in Turkish. Practice aloud. Spell out all numbers.

1. one half kilo of tea	20. three rivers
2. three kilos of sugar	21. seventy-seven lakes
3. two hundred grams of meat	22. three cities
	23. sixty-four boys
4. a slice of bread	24. one hundred children
5. two cups of coffee	25. one eye
6. eight apples	26. two eyes
7. How many houses?	27. two feet
8. two minarets	28. thirty-two teeth
9. one mosque	29. one head
10. three years	30. five hundred and fifty-five days
11. four days	
12. two weeks	31. fifteen years
13. six months	32. twelve girls
14. much milk	33. nineteen times
15. a little water	34. sixteen gardens
16. two loaves of bread	35. thirty-five nights
17. two slices of bread	36. thirty-six days
18. very little sugar	37. fifty-seven and a half grams
19. many trees	

38. one hundred liras
39. two and a half liras
40. two thousand kilowatts
41. many mosques
42. How many mosques?
43. a good many streets
44. much water

45. little water
46. How many glasses of water?
47. a little water
48. four times
49. much fruit
50. many apples

Lesson 3

Position of Adjectives. Indefinite Article
with Adjectives. Predicate Modifiers

---

1. Position of adjectives

büyük kız	(the) big girl
küçük kız	(the) little girl
genç adam	(the) young man
yaşlı kadın	(the) old woman (*yaşlı* 'old,' of humans; otherwise use *eski*)

When an adjective precedes a noun, it modifies that noun, as in English.

2. Indefinite article with adjectives

bir köpek	a dog; one dog
bir gün	a day; one day
bir elma	an apple; one apple
bir bardak su	a glass of water; one glass of water
büyük bir kız	a big girl
küçük bir kız	a little girl
çok küçük bir kız	a very little girl
iki çok küçük kız	two very little girls
küçük güzel kız	(the) little, pretty girl
küçük güzel bir kız	a little, pretty girl
küçük ve güzel bir kız	a little and pretty girl

The word *bir* serves as the number 'one' and as the indefinite article 'a,'
'an.' When the indefinite article and one or more other adjectives modify

one noun, Turkish reverses the English order. The adjective or adjectives come first, and the indefinite article immediately precedes the noun. When the word *bir* means 'one,' however, it precedes the adjective (or adjectives), as in English, e.g., *büyük bir kız* 'a big girl,' *bir büyük kız* 'one big girl.'

NOTE 1: Turkish sometimes uses *bir* with a plural noun. (See Lesson 4, section 5.)

NOTE 2: *Bir* may be omitted from a Turkish sentence in which the English would require the indefinite article. (See Lesson 14, section 1.)

3. Predicate modifiers

O kız uzun.	That girl is tall.
Bu kız kısa.	This girl is short.
Küçük kız güzel.	The little girl is pretty.
Güzel kız küçük.	The pretty girl is little.
Bu küçük kız çok güzel.	This little girl is very pretty.
Bu çok küçük kız güzel.	This very small girl is beautiful.
Bu kız çok küçük ve çok güzel.	This girl is very tiny and very pretty.
Bir kız uzun, bir kız kısa.	One girl is tall, (and) one girl is short.
Bu çay çok iyi.	This tea is very good.
Güzel kız uzun, diğer kız kısa.	The pretty girl is tall; the other girl is short.
Bu iyi.	This is good.

In speech (and to a lesser degree in the formal written language), the third person forms, singular and plural, present tense of the Turkish verb 'to be' are not expressed. Hence a Turkish adjective in the predicate position (i.e., following the noun it modifies) expresses a complete sentence, e.g., *O kız uzun* 'That girl (is) tall.'

Exercises

A. Practice aloud. Translate.

1. güzel bir anne
2. O anne güzel.
3. Çocuk çok uzun.
4. çok uzun bir çocuk

5. genç bir kız
6. Bir kız genç.
7. Genç kız küçük.
8. Bu genç kız çok küçük.

19

9. Bu iki kadın iyi.
10. on iki iyi kadın
11. Bu çok küçük.
12. iki yaşlı kadın
13. İki kadın yaşlı.
14. İki yaşlı kadın kısa.
15. Baba iyi.
16. bir iyi baba
17. iki iyi baba
18. İki baba iyi.
19. Kaç tane baba?
20. Kaç gün?
21. Kaç tane elma?
22. iyi bir gün
23. Bugün iyi.
24. Bu, iyi bir gün.
25. büyük otomobil
26. iki büyük otomobil
27. İki otomobil büyük.
28. Bu, küçük bir otomobil.
29. Bir otomobil yeni,
    diğer otomobil eski.
30. Büyük otomobil yeni.
31. Diğer otomobil çok eski.
32. Bu, çok eski.
33. Bu şeker iyi.
34. biraz şeker
35. O göl çok büyük.
36. iki güzel göl
37. İki göl güzel.
38. az para
39. Bu para çok az.
40. biraz para
41. üç fincan kahve
42. üç kahve
43. üç tane kahve
44. birçok fincan
45. birçok fincan çay
46. Kaç para?
47. otuz beş lira on beş
    kuruş
48. beş eski ev
49. Beş ev eski.
50. Bu çok eski.

B. Write in Turkish. Practice aloud.

1. a big foot
2. one big foot
3. two big feet
4. This foot is big.
5. One foot is large; the other
   foot is small.
6. How many women?
7. two old women
8. These two women are old.
9. The two old women are short.
10. two short old women
11. a nice street
12. two nice streets
13. This city is new; the other city
    is old.
14. three tall minarets
15. this old house
16. This house is high.
17. The old house is large;
    the new house is small.
18. How many houses?
19. How many small houses?
20. How many houses are
    small?
21. This house is very small.
22. The very small house is
    lovely.
23. four young men
24. The four men are young.
25. The four young men are tall.

Lesson 4

Definite Article.   Adjective and Noun.

Agglutination.   Vowel Harmony.   The Plural

---

küçük çocuk	(the) small child
Çocuk küçük.	(The) child (is) small.
büyük çocuk	(the) big child
Çocuk büyük.	(The) child (is) big.

---

1. Definite article

Turkish has no separate word equivalent to the English definite article 'the.' Hence any Turkish noun without suffixes (or with the plural suffix: see below, section 5) may be understood with or without 'the' as the sense requires.

> *baş*   head (or) the head   *kahve*   coffee (or) the coffee

NOTE: For the devices by which, in certain circumstances, Turkish specifies whether or not a noun is definite see Lesson 6, section 2.

2. Adjective and noun

When an adjective does not modify a noun, the adjective can become a substantive.

> **Bu genç çocuk güzel.** (*Genç* is used as an attributive adjective.) 'This young child is pretty.' **Bu anne genç.** (*Genç* is used as a predicate adjective.) 'This mother is young.'
>
> **Bu genç güzel.** (*Genç* is used as a substantive 'youth,' 'youngster.') 'This youngster is pretty.'

Such a word, when it is an adjective, takes no suffixes. Such a word, when it is a substantive, may take suffixes.

3. Agglutination

Turkish is said to be an agglutinative language because every element that is affixed to a word or to another element in order to convey meaning is a suffix. Turkish uses no prefixes, except for a few stereotyped borrowings from other languages.

4. Vowel harmony

The eight Turkish vowels are divided into two classes: (1) those formed toward the front of the mouth and (2) those formed toward the back. These classes are called front and back vowels, respectively.

FRONT VOWELS	BACK VOWELS
e	a
i	ı
ö	o
ü	u

NOTE: The vowels ö and o tend to occur only in the first syllable of an originally Turkish word. With few exceptions ö and o do not appear in suffixes.

Each originally Turkish word tends to have all its vowels of the same class, all front or all back. This phenomenon is called vowel harmony. Foreign words borrowed by Turkish, but not entirely assimilated into the language, do not always entirely conform to the principle of vowel harmony. (See Lesson 6, section 2.)

When a suffix is to be added to a word, the final vowel of the word determines the class of vowel (front or back) in that suffix. Therefore, the final vowel is called the dominant vowel. If still another suffix is to be added, the final vowel of the preceding suffix is considered the dominant vowel.

5. The plural

ev	(the) house	**fil**	(the) elephant
evler	(the) houses	**filler**	(the) elephants
dağ	(the) mountain	**yıl**	(the) year
dağlar	(the) mountains	**yıllar**	(the) years

göl	(the) lake	**gün**	(the) day
göller	(the) lakes	**günler**	(the) days
top	(the) ball	**pul**	(the) stamp
toplar	(the) balls	**pullar**	(the) stamps

The Turkish plural is formed by the addition to a noun of the plural suffix, which appears as *-ler* after a front dominant vowel (*e, i, ö, ü*) and as *-lar* after a back dominant vowel (*a, ı, o, u*). Thus the vowel of the plural suffix always conforms to the principle of vowel harmony.

The symbol V^2 denotes the variable vowel *e/a*. After a front dominant vowel V^2 is *e*; after a back dominant vowel, *a*. The plural suffix may be shown schematically as follows:

$$-l\ V^2\ r$$

(In this notation, the hyphen indicates that what follows is a suffix, not a word. The hyphen is not written after the suffix, but suffixes may be added to other suffixes.)

DOMINANT VOWEL FRONT				DOMINANT VOWEL BACK		
ev	house	**evler**	houses	**dağ**	mountain	**dağlar** mountains
fil	elephant	**filler**	elephants	**yıl**	year	**yıllar** years
göl	lake	**göller**	lakes	**top**	ball	**toplar** balls
gün	day	**günler**	days	**pul**	stamp	**pullar** stamps

NOTE 1: Each noun in the above table, whether in its singular or plural form, is to be understood as being nominative or 'absolute' so long as it bears no other suffix; hence each may be understood with or without the English definite article, as the sense requires.

NOTE 2: A few writers and printers insert an apostrophe between a noun and its (first) suffix. This apostrophe does not alter the pronunciation. It is most frequently used after foreign words and after place-names.

The indefinite article of course has no plural.

    bir ev   a house   **evler**   houses (the houses)

A common word for 'some' is *bazı* (followed by a substantive with a plural suffix).

    bir ev   a house   **bazı evler**   some houses

Bazı may infrequently be used with the singular.

    Bazı zaman   sometimes

Bir may infrequently be used with the plural.

    bir zamanlar   once upon a time

Exercises

A. Practice aloud. Translate.

1. Bugün güzel.
2. Bu günler güzel.
3. Bu fincanlar çok küçük.
4. Kaç tane küçük fincan?
5. Kaç tane fincan küçük?
6. Bazı fincanlar çok büyük.
7. O fincanlar güzel.
8. Beş fincan iyi kahve.
9. Bu genç çocuk çok büyük.
10. Bu genç çok uzun.
11. Bu genç çocuklar çok küçük.
12. Bu gençler çok kısa.
13. Bu fincan büyük.
14. Bu büyük fincan güzel.
15. Bu fincanlar güzel.
16. Bu büyük fincanlar güzel.
17. Büyükler güzel.
18. Bu büyükler çok iyi.
19. Bu ev küçük.
20. Bu küçük ev güzel.
21. Bu küçük evler güzel.
22. Küçükler çok güzel.
23. Küçükler eski, büyükler yeni.
24. Kaç tane ev küçük?
25. Kaç tane küçük ev?

B. Write in Turkish. Practice aloud.

1. one horse
2. one big horse
3. a big horse
4. big horses
5. the big horses
6. two big horses
7. some big horses
8. Some horses are big.
9. This big horse is very good.
10. The other big horse is very bad.
11. The two big horses are beautiful.
12. These horses are small.
13. The big ones are very good; the little ones are bad.
14. two old women
15. the two old women
16. some old women
17. some old ones
18. This woman is old; the other woman is young.
19. The old ones are little.
20. The young ones are good-looking.
21. Fahrünnisa is young; Ahmet is very old.
22. This is good.
23. This one is good.
24. The little houses are old; the large houses are new.
25. The little ones are old; the large ones are new.

Lesson 5

Common Infinitive. Variable Consonants.

Past Definite Verb. Agreement of Subject and Verb

---

1. **Gelmek çok kolay.**	Coming (to come) (is) extremely easy.
2. **Bilmek güç.**	Comprehension (knowing, to know) (is) difficult.
3. **Baktım.**	I looked (stared).
4. **Ben baktım.**	*I* looked (stared).
5. **Baktım baktım.**	I looked hard (stared and stared).
6. **Ben baktım baktım.**	*I* stared and stared.
7. **Ahmet geldi.**	Ahmet came.
8. **Geldi.**	He (she, it) came.
9. **Baktık.**	We have stared. (We stared.)
10. **Fahrünnisa gitti.**	Fahrünnisa has gone (went).
11. **Ahmet ve Mehmet geldiler.**	Ahmet and Mehmet came (have come).
12. **Onlar geldiler.**	*They* have come (came).
13. **Geldiler.**	They've come (came).
14. **Geldiler!**	They're here! (They've come!)
15. **Günler geçti.**	(The) days (have) passed.

---

1. Common infinitive

The common or normal infinitive is formed by adding the suffix

$$\text{-m } V^2 \text{ k}$$

to the simple verb. The simple verb (or 'naked' verb) is the singular imperative. (See Lesson 7, section 4.) The common infinitive is the verb form listed in a Turkish dictionary. Its meaning is rendered equally well in English, in the case of the common infinitive *gelmek*, by 'coming' (noun) or by 'to come.'

Common infinitives:

DOMINANT VOWEL FRONT		DOMINANT VOWEL BACK	
gelmek	coming, to come	**almak**	taking, to take
bilmek	knowing, to know	**kırmak**	breaking, to break (transitive)
görmek	seeing, to see	**olmak**	becoming, happening, to become, to happen
gülmek	laughing, to laugh	**bulmak**	finding, to find

2. Variable consonants

As noted above, Turkish is an agglutinative language. It avoids prefixes. Every Turkish element which is affixed to a word (or to another element) is a suffix. When a suffix is added to a word (or to a preceding suffix), two sorts of consonant change may occur.

a. The initial consonant of the newly added suffix may be altered.

b. The final consonant of the preceding word (or suffix) may be altered.

Three variable consonants (or three consonant pairs) are involved in such changes. They are shown by these symbols:

$$t/d \qquad p/b \qquad ç/c$$

In each case, the first component of the symbol is a voiceless consonant (a consonant which is produced without vibration of the vocal cords). The second component is the corresponding voiced consonant. (A voiced consonant is produced with vibration of the vocal cords.) Turkish voiceless consonants are: *ç, f, h, k, p, s, ş, t*. All other Turkish consonants are voiced.

CONSONANT CHANGES

Type 1: Initial consonant of newly added suffix changes.

When a suffix begins with the variable consonant *t/d* or with the variable consonant *ç/c* (no Turkish suffix begins with *p/b*), that initial variable consonant appears in its voiceless form when it is attached to a voiceless consonant, in its voiced form when it is attached to a directly preceding voiced sound (consonant or vowel).

süt	milk	**sütçü**	milkman
kahve	coffee	**kahveci**	coffeehouse keeper
ev	house	**evde**	in the house
ateş	fire	**ateşte**	in the fire

Type 2: Final consonant of preceding word (or suffix) changes.

26

When a word (or suffix) ends in one of the variable consonants, that final variable consonant appears in its voiceless form unless it is immediately followed by a suffixed vowel.

ağaç	(the) tree
ağaçta	in the tree
ağacı	the tree (objective definite)

NOTE 1: Many nouns of one syllable, and some nouns of more than one syllable, ending in *ç*, *p*, or *t*, do not change the final consonant to *c*, *b*, or *d* before an immediately suffixed vowel. Such instances are often indicated in dictionaries as: *top* (*-pu*) 'ball'; *et* (*-ti*) 'meat'; *sepet* (*-ti*) 'basket'; *üç* (*-çü*) 'three.'

NOTE 2: The consonant change in verb stems occurs only in a limited number of verbs. *Gitmek* (*gid-*), and *etmek* (*ed-*) are the only prominent examples in which the shift does occur.

3. Past definite verb

The past definite verb forms denote action which really was or really has been completed in the past. The past definite forms are obtained by adding to the verb stem (the 'naked' verb, the common infinitive minus its suffix, -m V^2 k) the following endings.

	SINGULAR	PLURAL
1st person	-t/d V^4 m	-t/d V^4 k
2nd person	-t/d V^4 n	-t/d V^4 n V^4 z
3rd person	-t/d V^4	-t/d V^4 l V^2 r

The symbol V^4 represents the four-variable vowel shown in the following table.

FRONT		BACK	
When dominant vowel is		When dominant vowel is	
e or *i*	$V^4 = i$	*a* or *ı*	$V^4 = ı$
ö or *ü*	$V^4 = ü$	*o* or *u*	$V^4 = u$

The symbol -*t/d* indicates that these suffixes begin with a variable consonant.

Study the verbs whose past definite forms are given below.

VERBS WHOSE DOMINANT VOWEL IS *a*

	verb stem ends in		
	VOICED CONSONANT	VOICELESS CONSONANT	VOWEL (VOICED)
common infinitive	**almak**	**bakmak**	**anlamak**
verb stem	**al**	**bak**	**anla**
meaning	taking, to take	looking, to look	understanding, to understand

singular			
1st person	aldım	baktım	anladım
2nd person	aldın	baktın	anladın
3rd person	aldı	baktı	anladı
plural			
1st person	aldık	baktık	anladık
2nd person	aldınız	baktınız	anladınız
3rd person	aldılar	baktılar	anladılar

All past definite forms express action that really is finished, really was or has been completed in the past. Hence the first person singular past definite of *almak*, the form *aldım* (of the verb which means 'taking,' 'getting possession of,' 'receiving,' 'acquiring') may mean any or all of the following, depending upon the particular context in which *aldım* is used.

I took	I got	I received
I did take	I did get	I did receive
I have taken	I have got	I have received

In the same way, the second singular form, *aldın*, means that you (one person) really did complete or have completed the action of taking, getting, receiving, acquiring something. Among possible translations for *aldın* are:

you (singular) took
you (singular) did take
you (singular) have taken

and so on for the words 'get,' 'acquire,' etc. The verb *satın almak* means 'to buy.'

NOTE SECOND PERSON SINGULAR AND PLURAL
The second person singular is used:
a. when speaking to a child or an inferior
b. as a token of familiarity or affection when speaking to an intimate
c. rudely as an insult to an individual
d. solemnly when addressing God or invoking a person who is dead

The second person plural is used:
a. when speaking to more than one person
b. as the normal, polite way to address one individual.

In the absence of an expressed subject, the third person singular form, *aldı*, is assumed to have for its subject the pronoun *o* 'he,' 'she,' or 'it.'

Aldı. He (she, it) took (did take, has taken something), or He (she, it) got (did get, has gotten something), or the same shades of past definite meaning for the verb 'acquire.'

28

Aldı may of course have an expressed subject. *Ahmet aldı.* 'Ahmet got, took, received,' etc.

The first plural past definite form, *aldık*, not only rings all the changes noted above ('we really did take, have taken,' etc.). In addition, since the first person plural is frequently used to mean 'I' (a sort of polite and modest editorial 'we'), the word *aldık* may also, if the context requires, express all the meanings given above for the first singular form, *aldım.*

Aldınız indicates that you (one or more persons [see the note above]) in the past definitely did perform or have performed the action of *almak*—taking, getting, acquiring, etc.

Aldılar shows that they (two or more persons) really did perform or have performed that action.

The second verb in the table—*bakmak*—expresses the action of looking, staring, and (with proper suffixes on the substantives concerned) of looking after, caring for, examining, etc. Thus *baktım baktım* (Turkish repeats words for emphasis) means

> I looked and looked.
> I did look and look.
> I have looked and looked.
> etc.

The third verb—*anlamak*—expresses the idea of comprehending, understanding, catching on, getting the point, etc. Thus its third plural past definite form, *anladılar*, may mean any of the following

> They really did understand, realize, comprehend, etc.
> have understood, etc.
> understood, etc.

NOTE: For *almak, bakmak, anlamak,* and indeed for most Turkish verbs, it is very misleading to try to give one English word which is what the Turkish word 'means.' Instead, the student should attach to the Turkish verb, or noun, or adjective a basic idea which has many possible shades of expression in English.

Each of the three verbs in the above table has the dominant vowel *a*: *almak* with a final voiced consonant (*al*), *bakmak* with a final voiceless consonant (*bak*), and *anlamak* (*anla*), with a vowel, which is also a voiced sound.

Here follow verbs whose dominant vowels are *e, ı, i, u, ü, o,* and *ö*. These tables are not complete: no exotic verbs are introduced simply for the sake of completion.

29

VERBS WHOSE DOMINANT VOWEL IS *e*

verb stem ends in

	VOICED CONSONANT	VOICELESS CONSONANT	VOWEL (VOICED)
common infinitive	*gelmek*	*çekmek*	*istemek*
verb stem	*gel*	*çek*	*iste*
meaning	coming, to come	pulling, to pull	wishing, wanting, needing, requiring, etc. to need

singular
1st person	**geldim**	**çektim**	**istedim**
2nd person	**geldin**	**çektin**	**istedin**
3rd person	**geldi**	**çekti**	**istedi**

plural
1st person	**geldik**	**çektik**	**istedik**
2nd person	**geldiniz**	**çektiniz**	**istediniz**
3rd person	**geldiler**	**çektiler**	**istediler**

VERBS WHOSE DOMINANT VOWEL IS *ı*

common infinitive	*kırmak*	*bıkmak*
verb stem	*kır*	*bık*
meaning	breaking, to break (trans.)	get tired of, have enough of, to tire of

singular
1st person	**kırdım**	**bıktım**
2nd person	**kırdın**	**bıktın**
3rd person	**kırdı**	**bıktı**

plural
1st person	**kırdık**	**bıktık**
2nd person	**kırdınız**	**bıktınız**
3rd person	**kırdılar**	**bıktılar**

VERBS WHOSE DOMINANT VOWEL IS *i*

common infinitive	*bilmek*	*itmek*
verb stem	*bil*	*it*
meaning	knowing, to know	pushing, to push

singular

1st person	**bildim**	**ittim**
2nd person	**bildin**	**ittin**
3rd person	**bildi**	**itti**

plural

1st person	**bildik**	**ittik**
2nd person	**bildiniz**	**ittiniz**
3rd person	**bildiler**	**ittiler**

VERBS WHOSE DOMINANT VOWEL IS *o*

common infinitive	*olmak*	*koşmak*
verb stem	*ol*	*koş*
meaning	becoming, happening, to become, to happen	running, to run

singular

1st person	**oldum**	**koştum**
2nd person	**oldun**	**koştun**
3rd person	**oldu**	**koştu**

plural

1st person	**olduk**	**koştuk**
2nd person	**oldunuz**	**koştunuz**
3rd person	**oldular**	**koştular**

VERBS WHOSE DOMINANT VOWEL IS *ö*

common infinitive	*görmek*	*öpmek*
verb stem	*gör*	*öp*
meaning	seeing, perceiving, to see, to perceive	kissing, to kiss

singular

1st person	**gördüm**	**öptüm**
2nd person	**gördün**	**öptün**
3rd person	**gördü**	**öptü**

plural

1st person	**gördük**	**öptük**
2nd person	**gördünüz**	**öptünüz**
3rd person	**gördüler**	**öptüler**

31

VERBS WHOSE DOMINANT VOWEL IS *u*

common infinitive	*bulmak*	*tutmak*	*okumak*
verb stem	*bul*	*tut*	*oku*
meaning	finding, to find	grasping, holding, to grasp, to hold	reading, to read
singular			
1st person	**buldum**	**tuttum**	**okudum**
2nd person	**buldun**	**tuttun**	**okudun**
3rd person	**buldu**	**tuttu**	**okudu**
plural			
1st person	**bulduk**	**tuttuk**	**okuduk**
2nd person	**buldunuz**	**tuttunuz**	**okudunuz**
3rd person	**buldular**	**tuttular**	**okudular**

VERBS WHOSE DOMINANT VOWEL IS *ü*

common infinitive	*gülmek*	*yürümek*
verb stem	*gül*	*yürü*
meaning	laughing, to laugh	walking, to walk
singular		
1st person	**güldüm**	**yürüdüm**
2nd person	**güldün**	**yürüdün**
3rd person	**güldü**	**yürüdü**
plural		
1st person	**güldük**	**yürüdük**
2nd person	**güldünüz**	**yürüdünüz**
3rd person	**güldüler**	**yürüdüler**

4. Agreement of subject and verb

Verb and subject agree in person and number. When the subject is a personal pronoun, the pronoun is not used unless special emphasis is desired.

normal expression	*Geldim.*	I came.
	Gördünüz.	You saw.
for emphasis	*Ben geldim.*	I came.
	Siz gördünüz.	You saw

With a third person plural subject which refers to animate beings, especially to humans, the verb is almost always in the third plural form, but may be third singular form.

Ahmet ve Mehmet geldiler.	Ahmet and Mehmet came.
Gençler koştular.	The youths ran.

Rarely

Ahmet ve Mehmet geldi.	Ahmet and Mehmet came.
Gençler koştu.	The youths ran.

In the case of a third plural subject which does not refer to animate beings, especially to humans, the situation is reversed: the verb usually is in the third singular form, but may be third plural form.

	Günler geçti.	(The) days passed.
	Atlar koştu.	The horses ran.
Sometimes		
	Atlar koştular.	The horses ran.

NOTE: Any of the above past definite forms may, of course, express any shade of action which really was, or has been, completed in the past. See Lesson 5, section 3.

Exercises

A. Practice aloud. Translate.

1. **Kim geldi?**
2. **Ne zaman geldiniz?**
3. **Çok okudular.**
4. **Az okudun.**
5. **Çok az anladım.**
6. **Az anladık.**
7. **Çocuklar çok koştular.**
8. **İki çocuk bu sabah geldiler.**
9. **Bu kahve çok iyi.**
10. **Bir buçuk kilo kahve satın aldım.**
11. **Kim güldü?**
12. **Erdoğan çok güldü.**
13. **Kaç defa geldiniz?**
14. **İstanbul büyük ve güzel bir şehir.**
15. **Akdeniz büyük, Marmara Denizi küçük.**
16. **Ev güzel bahçe büyük.**
17. **Gençler bugün geldiler.**
18. **Beş genç güldüler.**
19. **Bu çocuk çok genç.**
20. **Genç kız koştu.**
21. **iki büyük göz**
22. **İki göz büyük.**
23. **Bu göz büyük; o göz küçük.**
24. **Bu ne?**
25. **Bu bir elma.**
26. **Kaç litre süt?**
27. **iki buçuk fincan süt**
28. **Onlar kim?**
29. **Onlar Sait ve Ali.**

30. Kim anladı?
31. Onlar anladılar.
32. Bu evler büyük.
33. Bunlar büyük.
34. Büyükler bu sabah geldiler.
35. Gençler bu akşam geldiler.
36. Meyvalar oldu.
37. Ahmet gelmek istedi.
38. Ahmet, ne zaman geldin?
39. Bu sabah geldim.
40. Çocuklar biraz okudular.

41. Ne istediler?
42. Kaç otomobil gördünüz?
43. Beş otomobil gördüm.
44. Ne oldu?
45. iyi çocuklar
46. Ne zaman geldin?
47. Gençler koştular.
48. Ne buldunuz?
49. iki iyi çocuk
50. Ne okudular?

B. Write in Turkish. Practice aloud.

1. a big boy
2. The boy is big.
3. four little girls
4. The four girls are little.
5. five pretty little girls
6. These five little girls
   are pretty.
7. three big bad boys
8. A bad boy came this
   morning.
9. The bad boy came this
   morning.
10. Who came?
11. When did Ahmet come?
12. two kilos of oranges
13. two kilos of good oranges

14. These two kilos of oranges
    are very good.
15. The apples are very good;
    the oranges are bad.
16. Süheylâ has read much.
17. We took very little.
18. This city is very large.
19. The sea and mountains are lovely.
20. The street is big;
    the mosque is small.
21. When did they come?
22. How many apples did
    Ahmet want?
23. He wanted seven apples.
24. How many spoons of sugar?
25. How many slices of bread?

Lesson 6

Verbs of the Type *Gitmek* (*Gider*).

Objective Definite

---

1. **Geldi gitti.**	He's come (and) gone. (He came [and] went.)
2. **İstanbulu gördük.**	We've seen (been to) Istanbul.
3. **Kahveyi bu sabah satın aldım.**	I bought the coffee this morning.
4. **Ahmedi dün gördüm.**	I saw Ahmet yesterday.
5. **Köpek güzel.**	The dog's a fine one.
6. **Köpeği kim gördü?**	Who's seen the dog?
7. **Ben dün bir köpek gördüm.**	*I* saw a dog yesterday.
8. **Yalnız o adamı gördünüz.**	You saw only that man.
9. **Sizi gördüler.**	They saw you.
10. **Kaç kilo şeker aldı?**	How many kilos of sugar did he (or she) buy?

---

1. Verbs of the type *gitmek* (*gider*)

A few verbs—of which *gitmek* (*gider*), 'to go,' and *etmek* (*eder*), the auxiliary verb meaning 'to do,' are the most important—have stems which end in the variable consonant *t/d* (for *gitmek*, the stem is *git* or *gid*; for *etmek*, *et* or *ed*).

When a suffix whose own initial sound is also a variable consonant is added to a verb stem of this limited type, both the final variable consonant of the verb stem and also the initial variable consonant of the suffix appear in their voiceless forms.

35

A case in point is the past definite. The forms for *gitmek* and *etmek* are

singular

1st person	**ettim**	**gittim**	I went, did go, have gone, etc.
2nd person	**ettin**	**gittin**	
3rd person	**etti**	**gitti**	

plural

1st person	**ettik**	**gittik**
2nd person	**ettiniz**	**gittiniz**
3rd person	**ettiler**	**gittiler**

When, however, to a verb stem of this type there is added a suffix whose initial sound is a vowel, the final variable consonant of the verb stem appears in its voiced form. The third singular form of the general verb (see Lesson 11, section 2) illustrates this variation, e.g., for *gitmek*, the third singular general is *gider*; for *etmek*, it is *eder*.

Verbs of the type *gitmek* (*gider*) are sometimes shown in dictionaries by indicating the third singular general form in parentheses, after the common infinitive.

2. The objective definite

The objective definite suffix has a double function. It simultaneously indicates (a) that the substantive to which it is attached is the direct object of a verb, and (b) that the same substantive is definite. (A substantive is definite when it is the proper name of a person, place, or thing, or when, in English, the corresponding word is preceded by 'the,' a word indicating possession, or by a demonstrative adjective.) Unless the substantive in question meets the second of these conditions (i.e., is definite), it does not take this suffix, even though it is the direct object of a verb.

Hence, the objective suffix can be called a definite article that is used only with the objective. When attached to a word that ends in a consonant, this suffix is simply the variable vowel V^4, (*i, ı, ü, u*). When this suffix is attached to a word that ends in a vowel, however, a consonant buffer is needed between the word's terminal vowel and the V^4 of the suffix because Turkish abhors the sequence vowel–vowel (see Lesson 1, section 5). With the objective definite suffix, the buffer consonant employed is *y*. Hence the full notation for the objective definite suffix is

$$-(y) V^4$$

(In this notation, the hyphen shows that what follows is a suffix; the parentheses show that the *y* is a buffer consonant, employed only when it is needed; and the symbol V^4 indicates the four-variable vowel *i-ı-ü-u*.)

ABSOLUTE FORM		OBJECTIVE DEFINITE FORM
(The substantive may be (a) subject, definite or indefinite; or (b) object, indefinite.)		(The substantive is both (a) object and also (b) definite.)
gece	night	geceyi
geceler		geceleri
ev	house	evi
evler		evleri
efendi	gentleman, sir	efendiyi
efendiler		efendileri
fil	elephant	fili
filler		filleri
Mösyö	Monsieur	Mösyöyü
Mösyöler		Mösyöleri
göl	lake	gölü
göller		gölleri
sözcü	spokesman	sözcüyü
sözcüler		sözcüleri
gün	day	günü
günler		günleri
baba	father	babayı
babalar		babaları
dağ	mountain	dağı
dağlar		dağları
halı	rug	halıyı
halılar		halıları
yıl	year	yılı
yıllar		yılları
bando	band (musical)	bandoyu
bandolar		bandoları
top	ball	topu
toplar		topları
kutu	box	kutuyu
kutular		kutuları
pul	stamp	pulu
pullar		pulları

The sequence in which suffixes are added must always be learned by observation. In this case, for example, the plural suffix precedes the objective definite suffix. The objective definite is frequently used where English does not use a definite article (although English does, in these instances, convey the idea of definiteness).

> İzmiri gördük.   We have seen Izmir.
> Bizi gördüler.   They saw us.

Many words in common use (but not of Turkish origin) do not conform to vowel harmony, but are followed by front-voweled suffixes despite the presence of the back dominant vowel. This is sometimes shown in dictionaries in the following manner:

> **saat (saati)**   hour, time; watch, clock
> **hal (hali)**   circumstance, situation, condition

The form in parentheses is the objective definite.

3. Variable consonants followed by objective definite

In the case of words which end in a *ç*, *p*, or *t*, the terminal consonant of some nouns of one syllable and most nouns of more than one syllable assumes its voiced form before any immediately following vowel (see Lesson 5, section 2). This holds true with the objective definite suffix.

ABSOLUTE FORM		OBJECTIVE DEFINITE FORM
Ahmet	man's name	**Ahmedi**
Ahmetler		**Ahmetleri**
Mehmet	man's name	**Mehmedi**
Mehmetler		**Mehmetleri**
sahip	owner, master	**sahibi**
sahipler		**sahipleri**
ağaç	tree	**ağacı**
ağaçlar		**ağaçları**
dört	four	**dördü**
dörtler		**dörtleri**

Such words are shown in dictionaries with the objective definite form in parentheses, following the absolute form.

> *dört (dördü)*   four   *sahip (sahibi)*   owner, master

4. Doubled consonants followed by objective definite

Some originally non-Turkish words that in the original language end in a doubled consonant—for example, the Arabic word 'ḥaqq'—in their Turkish guise tend to drop the second consonant except when a vowel is directly suffixed. In that event, the doubled consonant reappears.

hak (hakkı)   right, truth; God

5. 'Ayn followed by objective definite

Many words which Turkish has borrowed from Arabic contained—in the original Arabic form—the characteristic Semitic consonant 'ayn (ﻉ). If any trace of the sound of this consonant remains in modern Turkish pronunciation, it is simply a full stop in the breath.

Turkish spelling does not indicate an original initial 'ayn.

Ali, man's name (Arabic 'Alî)

Turkish spelling may or may not indicate an original medial 'ayn.

> *sanat* or *san'at* 'art,' 'craft' (Arabic 'san'ah')
> Of these two possibilities, the first (*sanat*) may be pronounced with no stop in the breath; the second (*san'at*), with a full stop, indicated by the apostrophe.

Turkish spelling (and pronunciation) may or may not indicate an original final 'ayn. This is especially true when a vowel is directly suffixed to the word in question. *Cami* 'mosque' with the objective definite may appear as *camii* or as *camiyi*.

6. Final *k* followed by objective definite

Polysyllables in final *k* 'soften' that *k* to a *ğ* before an immediately suffixed vowel.

köpek (köpeği)	dog
elektrik (elektriği)	electricity
ayak (ayağı)	foot
bardak (bardağı)	drinking glass

Most monosyllables in final *k* do not soften the *k* to a *ğ* before an immediately following vowel.

ok (oku)	arrow

The word *çok* is an exception.

çok (çoğu)	much, many; lots (of)

7. Nouns of the type *oğul (oğlu)* followed by objective definite

Although Turkish admits a syllable of the pattern VCC (see Lesson 1, section 6), it frequently prefers to avoid the sequence consonant–consonant at the end of the final syllable of a substantive. Hence several nouns—some of them originally Turkish (*oğul* 'son') and some of them borrowed (*şehir* 'city' from Persian 'shahr')—whose absolute pattern would end with VCC, insert an 'unstable' vowel between the two final consonants. When an immediately following vowel is suffixed, however, the 'unstable' vowel drops out.

ABSOLUTE FORM		OBJECTIVE DEFINITE FORM
oğul	son	oğlu
oğullar		oğulları
şehir	city	şehri
şehirler		şehirleri

Nouns of the type *oğul* (*oğlu*) are so indicated in dictionaries.

Exercises

A. Practice aloud. Translate.

1. **Parayı kim aldı?**
   Parayı Ahmet aldı.
   Onu Ahmet aldı.
2. **Parayı kim aldı?**
   Ahmet aldı.
   Onu ne zaman aldı?
   Parayı bu sabah aldı.
   Onu bu sabah aldı.
   Bu sabah aldı.
3. **Mehmet, Ahmedi ne zaman**
   gördünüz?
   Ahmedi bugün gördüm.
   Bugün gördüm.
4. **Çocuklar! Bugün kimi**
   gördünüz?
   Bugün bir kaç adam gördük.
5. **Bu iki adamı kim gördü?**
   Onları biz gördük.
6. **Bu küçük kız ne kırdı?**
   Bir fincan kırdı.
7. **Fincanları kim kırdı?**
   Fincanları küçük kız kırdı.
   Onları küçük kız kırdı.

8. **Kız fincanları ne zaman kırdı?**
   Onları bu sabah kırdı.
9. **Küçük kız kaç tane fincan kırdı?**
   İki tane fincan kırdı.
   İki tane kırdı.
10. **Köpek neyi gördü?**
    Köpek kediyi gördü.
    Kedi koştu.
11. **Kedi ne istedi?**
    Kedi süt istedi.
    Kedi neyi buldu?
    Kedi sütü buldu.
12. **Bu beş bardağı kim aldı?**
    Onları ben aldım.
    Bardakları ne zaman aldınız?
    Bardakları bu akşam aldım.
13. **Bu dağlar çok güzel.**
    Güzel dağları gördüler.
    Bazı güzel dağlar gördüler.
14. **Ahmet, ne zaman geldin?**
    Bu sabah geldim.
    Ahmet ne zaman geldi?
    Bu sabah geldi.

15. Mehmet ve Sait dün
    geldiler.
    Dün kim geldi?
    Dün onlar geldiler.
16. Onu kim anladı?
    Onu ben anladım.
17. Geç geldiniz, Ahmet!
    Evet, çok geç geldim.

18. İstanbul büyük bir şehir.
    İstanbulu kim gördü?
    Onu biz gördük.
19. O çocuklar çok küçük.
    Ne zaman gittiler?
    Küçükler bu sabah gittiler.
20. Hoş geldiniz, Ahmet!
    Hoş bulduk, Mehmet!

B. Write in Turkish. Practice aloud.
1. I read the book yesterday.
2. I read two books yesterday.
3. Who has read this book?
4. You went yesterday.
5. Welcome, Fahrünnisa!
6. Thank you, I'm glad to be
   here, Selma!

7. Mehmet wanted some
   money.
8. How much money did
   Mehmet want?
9. Who wanted the money?
10. I found the two liras.

Lesson 7

Personal Pronouns. Interrogative Pronouns.

Demonstratives. The Imperative. Word Order

---

1. **Gel! Bunu al!**	Come here! Take this! (to one person, speaking most familiarly)
2. **Gelin! Bunu alın!**	Come here! Take this! (to one person, speaking less familiarly than above)
3. **Geliniz! Bunu alınız!**	Come here! Take this! (to one person, speaking formally, or to more than one person)
4. **Gelsin! Bunu alsın!**	Let him (her, it) come here! Let him (her, it) take this! (If only he would . . . I wish that he would . . . It would be a good thing if he would . . ., etc.)
5. **Gelsinler! Bunu alsınlar!**	If only they would come (and) take this! Let them come! Let them take this!
6. **Ben sizi gördüm, siz onları gördünüz.**	I saw you and you saw them.
7. **Sizi ben gördüm, onları siz gördünüz.**	*I* saw you and *you* saw them.

---

1. Personal pronouns

	ABSOLUTE (NOMINATIVE) FORM	OBJECTIVE DEFINITE FORM
singular		
1st person	**ben**	**beni**

2nd person	**sen**		**seni**
3rd person	**o**		**onu**
plural			
1st person	**biz**		**bizi**
2nd person	**siz**		**sizi**
3rd person	**onlar**		**onları**

Note that the buffer consonant with the third singular is *n* rather than the usual *y*, and that *n* precedes the plural suffix in the third plural forms.

Sometimes a plural suffix is used with the first and second plural forms.

> *bizler*   we   *sizler*   you

2. Interrogative pronouns

		OBJECTIVE DEFINITE	
ABSOLUTE FORM		FORM	
kim?	who?	**kimi?**	whom?
ne?	what?	**neyi?**	what?

These words sometimes take plural suffixes.

> *kimler*   *neler*

NOTE 1: *Ne* is sometimes an adjective.
> *ne zaman?*   when? (what time?)

NOTE 2: *Ne* is sometimes exclamatory.
> *ne güzel!*   how lovely!

3. Demonstratives

	ABSOLUTE FORM			OBJECTIVE DEFINITE FORM
singular				
1st person	**bu**	this		**bunu**
2nd person	**şu**	that		**şunu**
3rd person	**o**	that		**onu**
plural				
1st person	**bunlar**	these		**bunları**
2nd person	**şunlar**	those		**şunları**
3rd person	**onlar**	those		**onları**

Note that *o* 'that' is the same as *o* 'he,' 'she,' 'it.'

The basic distinction between *şu* 'that' and *o* 'that' is:

> *şu* refers to some thing, person, etc., that, although at some distance

from the speaker, is still within sight and can be indicated by a gesture;

o refers to some thing, person, etc., that is usually not in sight;

şu frequently means 'the following,' 'as follows.'

The demonstratives are adjectives when they modify a following noun, pronouns when used alone. As adjectives they take no suffixes. As pronouns they take suffixes. (Note the buffer *n*.)

From the demonstratives are formed the words

böyle	in this fashion, thus
şöyle	in that fashion, as follows
öyle	in that fashion

These words may be used adverbially or adjectivally.

Böyle oldu.	It happened in this fashion.
böyle bir gün	a day like this

4. The imperative

The Turkish imperative includes two persons.

a. the second person, singular and plural, the individual (or individuals) to whom one gives a command. '(you) come here!'

b. the third person, singular and plural, the individual or individuals about whom a sort of command is given. 'Let him come!' 'Let them take!'

'Please' is *lûtfen*.

The imperative suffixes are

singular

2nd person, Form I	verb stem without suffix
2nd person, Form II	verb stem plus (y) V^4 n
3rd person	verb stem plus s V^4 n

plural

2nd person	verb stem plus (y) V^4 n V^4 z
3rd person	verb stem plus s V^4 n l V^2 r

	gelmek	*almak*	*gitmek*	*istemek*
	to come	to take	to go	to want, wish
singular				
2nd person, Form I	**gel**	**al**	**git**	**iste**
2nd person, Form II	**gelin**	**alın**	**gidin**	**isteyin**
3rd person	**gelsin**	**alsın**	**gitsin**	**istesin**

plural

2nd person	**geliniz**	**alınız**	**gidiniz**	**isteyiniz**
3rd person	**gelsinler**	**alsınlar**	**gitsinler**	**istesinler**

The use of the second person singular and of the second plural has been presented (see Lesson 5, section 3).

In the second singular imperative, Form I (the simple verb stem) is ordinarily used. Form II (with the suffix -(y) V^4 n) expresses a degree of politeness between the familar Form I and the formal second plural. It is not frequently used, the second plural imperative or the second plural general (aorist) are preferred instead (see Lesson 11, section 2).

5. Word order

Word order in a formal Turkish sentence usually is

a. subject (unless the subject is an unexpressed personal pronoun)

b. object or complement (a pronoun object whose sense is clear is often left out where English would always express the object)

c. verb.

When the sentence includes an indirect object (shown by the dative suffix: see Lesson 8, section 2), the indirect object may precede or follow the direct object.

Generally speaking, the word immediately before the verb is the word whose position in the sentence gives it the greatest importance.

A comma frequently follows the subject.

Exercises

A. Practice aloud. Translate.

1. Ahmet otomobili aldı.
2. Otomobili Ahmet aldı.
3. Beni kim gördü?
4. Seni istediler.
5. Şu kitabı okudum fakat siz bunu okudunuz.
6. Büyük camii gördük. (Büyük camiyi gördük.)
7. Kimi istediler?
8. Mehmet, bak bak! Ahmet geldi.

9. Lûtfen, bu meyvayı alınız.
10. Kahveyi iç!
11. Gel, Mehmet! Ahmet bir şey kırdı.
12. Bunu anlamak çok güç.
13. Bizi kaç defa gördünüz?
14. Onlar ne zaman geldiler?
15. Onları bulunuz.
16. Dün bildin.
17. Böyle bir şeyi kim istedi?
18. Gittim, gördüm, geldim.

45

19. **Bu kitabı bugün okuyunuz, lûtfen.**

20. **Çabuk gelsinler!**

B. Write in Turkish. Practice aloud.

1. Find it!
2. Laugh!
3. He saw me and I saw him.
4. Let them come!
5. These are big.
6. I have seen Izmir and Eskişehir.
7. The big ones are these.
8. The boy came yesterday.
9. They went this week.
10. This month is very lovely.
11. He wanted 15 liras and 35 kuruş.
12. I received the 15 liras yesterday.
13. They bought two big rugs.
14. This is very difficult.
15. These things are very easy.

Lesson 8

Nere*, *Bura**, *Ora**. Dative, Locative, and Ablative.
Fractions. Calendar. The Word -d V^2

---

1. **Parayı nerede buldunuz?**	Where did you find the money?
2. **Kutuda buldum.**	I found (it) in the box.
3. **Parayı kime verdiniz?**	To whom did you give the money?
4. **Onu Ahmede verdim.**	I gave it to Ahmet.
5. **Parayı kimden aldınız?**	From whom did you get the money?
6. **Mehmetten aldık.**	We got it from Mehmet.

---

1. *Nere**, *Bura**, *Ora**

In the English sentences

a.	b.	c.
Where are you going?	Where is she?	Where did he come from?
I went there.	We were there.	He came from there.
They came here.	He is here.	They left here.

each of the words 'where,' 'there,' and 'here' expresses three distinct ideas.
a. place towards which   b. place in which   c. place from which

In Turkish, these three distinct ideas are indicated by distinct suffixes (the dative, locative, and ablative suffixes), and the three Turkish words *nere** 'where?' (interrogative), *bura** 'here,' 'this place,' and *ora** 'there,' 'that place' themselves take those suffixes.

The asterisks with *nere**, *bura**, and *ora** indicate that the absolute forms (the forms with no suffix) of these words do not occur in modern literary Turkish.

2. Dative suffix -(y) V²

The suffix -(y) V² denotes motion toward a point, motion through space or motion through time.

When it is attached to a word which ends in a variable consonant, that consonant assumes its voiced form.

ağaç	(the) tree	**ağaca**	to (the) tree
ağaçlar	(the) trees	**ağaçlara**	to (the) trees

In polysyllables, the dative suffix 'softens' a final *k* to *ğ*.

çocuk	(the) child	**çocuğa**	to (the) child
çocuklar	(the) children	**çocuklara**	to (the) children

With such verbs as *vermek* 'to give,' the dative suffix expresses the indirect object.

> **Kutuyu Ahmede verdi.**   He gave the box to Ahmet.

The dative suffix also denotes the recipient of the action of many verbs.

Ona güldü.	He laughed at it.
gülmek	to laugh, laugh at (with dative)
Bize baktılar.	They looked at us. They looked after us.
bakmak	to look at (with dative), to look after (with dative)

Verbs which govern a dative suffix on a preceding substantive are so noted in some dictionaries.

Another common function of the dative suffix is to express cause.

neye, alternative and more common form: **niye**   for what? why?

3. Locative suffix -t/d V²

This suffix -t/d V² denotes location at a point, a point in space or in time. When it is attached to a word ending in a variable consonant, that final variable consonant assumes its voiceless form as does the initial variable consonant of the suffix.

ağaç	(the) tree
ağaçta	at (the) tree
	in (the) tree
ağaçlar	(the) trees
ağaçlarda	in (the) trees
	at (the) trees

4. Ablative suffix -t/d V² n

This suffix -t/d V² n denotes motion away from a point, a point in space or in time. It affects a preceding variable consonant as does the locative suffix.

ağaç	(the) tree
ağaçtan	from (the) tree
ağaçlar	(the) trees
ağaçlardan	from (the) trees

Principal meanings of the ablative suffix include

a. cause

ondan	from that, because of that, therefore
neden	from what? why?

b. composition

taştan	from stone (*taş*), made out of stone
taştan bir ev	a stone house

c. the agent of the passive (see Lesson 21, section 2)

d. comparison (see Lesson 12, section 4)

e. the recipient of the action of such verbs as *bahsetmek* (the auxiliary verb *etmek* 'to do,' may be written as an enclitic, especially after a monosyllable), 'to speak of, about' (with ablative), 'to discuss' with ablative). Verbs which govern an ablative suffix on a preceding substantive are so noted in some dictionaries.

Onlardan çok bahsettik.	We talked a lot about them.
	We discussed them at length.

f. an adverbial sense

eskiden	of old, in olden times, formerly

Note such expressions as

birdenbire	suddenly (lit. 'from one to one')
doğrudan doğruya	directly, straightaway
	(lit. 'from straight to straight')

5. Dative, locative, and ablative forms of *nere**, *bura**, *ora**, the personal pronouns, the interrogatives, and the demonstratives *nere**, *bura**, *ora**, *şura**

nere*	what place?	**nerede**	at what place
nereye	to where?	**nereden**	from where?

bura*	this place	orada	at that place
buraya	to here	oradan	from there
burada	at this place	şura*	that place
buradan	from here	şuraya	to there
ora*	that place	şurada	at that place
oraya	to there	şuradan	from there

The above words sometimes take the plural suffix, e.g., *buralarda* 'in these parts.'

PERSONAL PRONOUNS

ben	I	siz	you (plural)
bana	to me	size	
bende	at (or) with me	sizde	
benden	from me	sizden	
biz	we	o	he, she, it; that
bize	to us	ona	
bizde	at (or) with us	onda	
bizden	from us	ondan	
sen	you (singular)	onlar	they
sana		onlara	
sende		onlarda	
senden		onlardan	

DEMONSTRATIVES

bu	this	şu	that
buna		şuna	
bunda		şunda	
bundan		şundan	
bunlar	these	şunlar	those
bunlara		şunlara	
bunlarda		şunlarda	
bunlardan		şunlardan	

INTERROGATIVES

kim	who?	ne	what?
kime		neye, niye	
kimde		nede	
kimden		neden	
kimler		neler	
kimlere		nelere	
kimlerde		nelerde	
kimlerden		nelerden	

6. Fractions

The locative is used in expressing fractions.

3te 2 (üçte iki)	2/3, in three, two
100de 15 (yüzde on beş)	15/100, 15 percent
yüzde yüz	100 percent

In addition to *dörtte bir* 'one fourth,' one may in certain situations use the word *çeyrek*, 'quarter.'

bir çeyrek saat	a quarter of an hour

7. Calendar

The days of the week are

Pazar	Sunday	**Perşembe**	Thursday
Pazartesi	Monday	**Cuma**	Friday
Salı	Tuesday	**Cumartesi**	Saturday
Çarşamba	Wednesday		

The names of the days are usually used in the possessive construction with the noun *gün* 'day' (see Lesson 10).

Pazar günü	Monday	**Salı günü**	Wednesday
Pazartesi günü	Tuesday		etc.

The months of the year are

Ocak	January (older terms are *İkinci Kânun* and *Son Kânun*)	**Ekim**	October (older terms are *Birinci Teşrin* and *İlk Teşrin*)
Şubat	February	**Kasım**	November (older terms are *İkinci Teşrin* and *Son Teşrin*)
Mart	March		
Nisan	April		
Mayıs	May		
Haziran	June	**Aralık**	December (older terms are *Birinci Kânun* and *İlk Kânun*)
Temmuz	July		
Ağustos	August		
Eylûl	September		

Nouns of time such as those above are often used absolutely (i.e., with no suffixes).

Salı günü	on Tuesday
bu ay	this month

8. The word d V²

This word must be distinguished from the locative suffix (-t/d V²; see Lesson 8, section 3).

The word d V² ('also,' 'too,' 'for X's part,' 'in X's turn'), although it is an independent word, conforms in vowel harmony to the preceding word.

Erdoğan da geldi.	Erdoğan came, too.
evde de	also in the house
garajlarda da	in (the) garages, too.

Repeated, d V² means 'both . . . and'

sana da bana da	to both you and me
senden de benden de	from both you and me

Exercises

A. Practice aloud. Translate.
 1. Dün sabah Ankaradan kaç kişi geldi?
    Beş kişi geldi.
    Nereden geldiler?
    Ankaradan.
    Ahmet ve Mehmet de geldiler.
    Evet, onlar da geldiler.
 2. Bu halılar çok güzel, Ali.
    Evet, çok güzel.
    Onları nerede buldunuz?
    Onları İstanbulda buldum.
    Nerede?
    Kapalıçarşıda.
    Onları kaça aldınız?
    Büyük halıya 500 lira verdim.
 3. Salı günü Ahmet Bey İstanbula geldi. Kapalıçarşıya gitti. Orada çok şey gördü. İki güzel halı satın aldı. Sonra Taksime gitti. O akşam Taksimde bir otelde kaldı. Çarşamba sabah saat sekizde İstanbuldan Ankaraya döndü.
 4. Kız dün İzmire gitti.
 5. Nereden geldi?
 6. Ankaradan geldi.
 7. Ahmedi nerede gördünüz?
 8. Köpek nerede?
 9. Köpeği bahçede gördüm.

10. Bir gün bir kedi bir köpek gördü. Köpek kediyi gördü. Kedi köpeğe baktı, baktı. Birdenbire kedi bahçeden kaçtı. Çabuk kaçtı. Köpek bahçeden eve döndü.
11. Parayı kimden aldılar?
12. Parayı Mehmetten aldılar.
13. Kaç para aldılar?
14. Ahmet on beş lirayı kime verdi?
15. Parayı onlara verdi.
16. Sütü kim içti?
17. Neyi içtiniz?
18. Anne ve baba Ahmetten bahsettiler.
19. Çok geç geldiniz.
20. Evet, geç geldik.

B. Write in Turkish. Practice aloud.

1. I also wanted that book.
2. Ahmet returned on Sunday.
3. Whom did they see in Izmir?
4. How many kilos of cheese did she want?
5. She wanted 250 grams of cheese.
6. This cheese is very good.
7. Where did they go yesterday?
8. Where did you come from this morning?
9. Who looked after the children?
10. Selma took care of them yesterday.
11. What did you see in the tree, Erdoğan?
12. I saw the cat in the tree, Father.
13. What did you find in the box, Ahmet?
14. I found ten liras in the box.
15. Who took the sugar out of the cup?

Lesson 9

Negative Verb. Interrogative Particle (m V⁴).

Negative Interrogative. Negative Expressions

---

1. Ahmet **Dün İstanbula gittiniz mi?**
Did you go to Istanbul yesterday?

   Mehmet **Hayır, gitmedim. Fakat Erdoğan gitti.**
No, I didn't. But Erdoğan did.

   A. **Niçin gitmediniz?**
Why didn't you go?

   M. **İstemedim.**
I didn't want to.

2. Selma **Peynir satın almadınız mı?**
Didn't you buy (any) cheese?

   Mihri **Almadım.**
No, I didn't.

   S. **Hiç bir şey satın almadınız mı?**
Didn't you buy anything?

   M. **Süt, kahve ve şeker satın aldım.**
I bought milk and coffee and sugar.

3. Ali **Ahmet parayı bulmadı mı?**
Didn't Ahmet find the money?

   Sait **Bulmadı.**
No, he didn't.

   A. **Onu siz buldunuz mu?**
Did you find it?

   S. **Hayır, ben de bulmadım.**
No, I didn't find it either.

4. Anne   **Köpeği gördün mü?**
             Have you seen the dog?

Kız   **Hayır, köpeği görmedim. Sen de onu görmedin mi?**
             No, I haven't seen the dog. Haven't you seen him either?

A.   **Ben de görmedim. Kediyi nerede gördün?**
             I haven't either. Where did you see the cat?

K.   **Kediyi de görmedim. Onu sen de görmedin mi?**
             I haven't seen the cat either. Haven't you seen her either?

1. Negative verb (-m V²)

The negative sign (or particle or syllable) is -m V². It is attached directly to the verb stem, and other suffixes are added to it.

COMMON INFINITIVE

POSITIVE		NEGATIVE	
gitmek	going, to go	**gitmemek**	not going, not to go
almak	taking, to take	**almamak**	
istemek	desiring, to want, to need	**istememek**	

NOTE: The syllable preceding the negative sign receives a distinct stress accent.

PAST DEFINITE NEGATIVE VERB FORMS

gitmedim	**almadım**	**istemedim**
gitmedin	**almadın**	**istemedin**
gitmedi	**almadı**	**istemedi**
gitmedik	**almadık**	**istemedik**
gitmediniz	**almadınız**	**istemediniz**
gitmediler	**almadılar**	**istemediler**

(For meanings, see the positive forms, Lesson 5, section 3.)

NEGATIVE IMPERATIVE FORMS

gitme	**alma**	**isteme**
gitmeyin	**almayın**	**istemeyin**
gitmesin	**almasın**	**istemesin**
gitmeyiniz	**almayınız**	**istemeyiniz**
gitmesinler	**almasınlar**	**istemesinler**

(For meanings, see the positive forms, Lesson 7, section 4.)

2. Interrogative particle (m V⁴)

Turkish possesses a spoken question mark, the interrogative particle m V⁴. Although it conforms in vowel harmony to the preceding word, this interrogative sign is not suffixed but is an independent word to which other suffixes may be added.

The syllable before the interrogative sign receives a distinct stress accent. There is no interrogative form of the infinitive.

PAST DEFINITE INTERROGATIVE VERB FORMS

buldum mu?	istedim mi?
buldun mu?	istedin mi?
buldu mu?	istedi mi?
bulduk mu?	istedik mi?
buldunuz mu?	istediniz mi?
buldular mı?	istediler mi?

The second person imperatives have no interrogative forms. Those for the third person imperatives are

Gelsin. Let him come. It would be a good idea if he were to come.

Gelsin mi? Should he come? Wouldn't it be a good idea for him to come?

Gelsinler.

Gelsinler mi?

The interrogative sign may follow other words besides verb forms,

Geldi mi?	Did he come?
O mu geldi?	Was it *he* who came?
Dün geldi mi?	Did he come yesterday?
Dün mü geldi?	Did he come *yesterday*?
Dün o mu geldi?	Was it *he* who came yesterday?

3. Negative interrogative verb

PAST DEFINITE, NEGATIVE INTERROGATIVE VERB FORMS

bulmadım mı?	istemedim mi?
bulmadın mı?	istemedin mi?
bulmadı mı?	istemedi mi?
bulmadık mı?	istemedik mi?
bulmadınız mı?	istemediniz mi?
bulmadılar mı?	istemediler mi?

gelmesin mi?
gelmesinler mi?

4. Negative expressions

The word *ne*, in addition to being the interrogative 'what?' and an exclamatory word 'how very!' (*ne güzel!* 'how lovely!'; *ne büyük!* 'how large!'), also has a negative use: *ne ... ne* 'neither ... nor.' When *ne ... ne* appears in a negative expression, the verb is positive.

ne sen ne ben	neither you nor I
Ne sen gittin, ne ben (gittim).	Neither you nor I went.
Ne Ahmedi ne Mehmedi gördüm.	I saw neither Ahmet nor Mehmet.

NOTE: *Ne* sometimes serves as an interrogative (**ne zaman?** 'what time?' 'when?'), but the usual interrogative is *hangi* 'which (one)?'

hangi gün?	which day? what day?
hangi kız?	which girl? what girl?

Hiç means 'none,' 'nothing.' *Hiç bir* means 'not a.' With these negative words, a negative verb is used.

Hiç bir şey istemedi.	He didn't want anything.

Hiç also means 'never.'

Kız hiç gülmedi.	The girl never laughed. The girl didn't laugh at all.
Hiç gitmedi mi?	Didn't he go at all? Did he never go? Didn't he ever go?

With a positive interrogative verb, *hiç* means 'ever.'

Hiç İstanbula gittiniz mi?	Have you ever been to Istanbul?

Exercises

A. Practice aloud. Translate.

1. Ahmet! Sen bugün mektebe gitmedin mi?
2. Hayır, baba. Bugün mektebe gitmedim.
3. Şehre gittin mi?
4. Hayır, baba. Bugün ne mektebe gittim ne de şehre.
5. O halde nereye gittin? Ne yaptın?
6. Bir bahçe gördüm. Bahçeye girdim.
7. Hangi bahçeye girdin?
8. Büyük bahçeye gitmedim. Küçük bahçeye girdim.

57

9. İzmire gittiniz mi? Orada ne kadar kaldınız?
   Orada iki, iki buçuk ay kaldım.
10. Ahmet, iyi çocuk ol! Mektebe git! Her gün git! Çok çok çalış! Anladın mı?
    Anlamadın mı?
    Anladım, baba, anladım.
11. Hiç Ankaraya gittiniz mi?
    Hayır, oraya hiç gitmedim. Çok gitmek istedim, fakat gitmedim.
    Ben Bursaya bile hiç gitmedim. Yalnız bir şehir gördüm—İstanbul.
    Siz Ankaraya gittiniz mi?
    Evet, oraya çok gittim. İzmire gittim. Adanaya da gittim . . .
12. Adanaya kaç defa gittiniz?
    Adanaya mı? Oraya beş altı defa gittim.
    Demek siz çok seyahat ettiniz.
    Evet, çok seyahat ettim.
13. Ankarayı nasıl buldunuz? Güzel mi?
    Evet, Ankara güzel.
    Ya İstanbul?
    İstanbul mu? O da güzel, çok güzel.
14. Bugün nereden geldiniz?
    Bugün Adanadan geldim.
    Oraya hangi gün gittiniz?
    Oraya Cumartesi günü gittim.
    Adanayı nasıl buldunuz?
    Çok büyük ve çok güzel. Fakat sıcak!
15. Onlar sizden para istediler mi, istemediler mi?
    İstediler, iki yüz yetmiş beş lira istediler.
    İki yüz yetmiş beş lirayı onlara verdiniz mi, vermediniz mi?
    Vermemek istedim, fakat verdim. Dün Ahmet bana üç yüz lira verdi.
    Bugün onlara iki yüz yetmiş beş lirayı verdim.

B. Write in Turkish. Practice aloud.
   1. Has Ahmet gone?
   2. Was it Ahmet who went?
   3. Did they give you the book? No, they didn't.
   4. Has Selma seen the two boys? Yes, she has.
   5. Why didn't you give us the money? Didn't you want to?
   6. I gave the money to Erdoğan yesterday. Haven't you seen him?
   7. Should they come or not?
   8. Why shouldn't Ahmet come?

9. She drank neither coffee nor tea.
10. Fahrünnisa drank nothing at all.
11. Did they ever go to Ankara?
12. Have you ever been to Ankara?
13. Did they come from Izmir?
14. No, they didn't come from there. They came from Adana.
15. Have you given Father the newspaper?
16. Yes, I have given it to him.
17. What did you find in the room?
18. I didn't find anything there.
19. Don't let him put either the cheese or the sugar into that box!
20. Should Ahmet read the newspaper or not?

Lesson 10

The Possessive Construction

1. çocuğum	my child
2. oğlun	your son
3. oğlu	his son
4. Ahmedin oğlu	Ahmet's son
5. çocuklarımız	our children
6. oğlunuz	your son
7. oğullarınız	your sons
8. Ahmedin oğulları	Ahmet's sons
9. çocuğumun kitabı	my child's book
10. Çocuğumun kitabını kim aldı?	Who took my son's book?
11. oğlunun kitapları	your son's books
12. Oğlunun kitaplarını hiç görmedik.	We have never seen your son's books.
13. Ahmedin oğlunun kitapları nerede?	Where are Ahmet's boy's books?
14. Ahmedin oğullarının büyük kitabını nereye koydular?	Where have they put the big book of Ahmet's sons?
15. radyo sahibi	radio owner
16. radyonun sahibi	owner of the radio
17. O adam ev sahibi mi?	Is that man (a) house owner?
18. Bu evin sahibi o adam mı?	Is the owner of this house that man?
19. Ankara Bulvarı İstanbulda mı?	Is Ankara Boulevard in Istanbul?
20. Ankaranın bulvarları ne güzel!	Ankara's main streets are certainly lovely!
21. Ev sahibinizin radyosunu kimin otomobiline koydular?	Whose car did they put your landlord's radio into?

1. The possessive construction

In possession, two elements are involved: A—the possessor; and B—what is possessed.

A	B	B	A
John's	book	the book of	John

In Turkish, the two substantives (A and B) are 'welded' into a grammatical relationship. They always stand in the order A—B. The first substantive A (the possessor) is here termed 'first member.' The second substantive B (the thing possessed) is termed the 'second member.'

The essential element which always joins the two members is a suffix added to the second member. This is here called the possessive suffix.

Still another suffix may be essential to the possessive construction. This suffix is added to the first member and is called the possessive definite suffix.

Hence the technical terms which the student should bear in mind in order to understand the possessive construction are:

1. first member — possessor (A), to this a suffix may be added
2. second member — thing possessed (B), to this a suffix must be added
3. possessive definite suffix — suffix which may be added to first member
4. possessive suffix — suffix which must be added to second member
5. possessive construction — possessor (A), thing possessed (B), and the suffixes as required by the situation.

Those possessive constructions whose first members bear the possessive definite suffix are here called Type I. Those possessive constructions whose first members bear no possessive definite suffix are called Type II. Ordinarily, no word may intervene between the first and second members of a Type II construction. Words may intervene between the members of a Type I construction.

2. Possessive definite suffix: -(n) V^4 n

This suffix -(n) V^4 n is added directly to the singular or plural. Its meaning is that of English *'s* attached to a definite substantive, but this suffix is not the essential element in the Turkish expression of possession. Instead, it shows that the possessor is definite.

ev	(the) house	**halı**	(the) rug
evin	the house's	**halının**	the rug's
evlerin	the houses'	**halıların**	the rugs'
ayak	(the) foot	**bu**	this (substantive)
ayağın	the foot's	**bunun**	of this
ayakların	the feet's	**bunların**	of these

The pronoun forms are

benim (note the first person suffix) my		**bizim** (note the first person suffix) our	
senin	your	**sizin**	your
onun	his, her, its	**onların**	their

The buffer consonant with *su* 'water' is *y* rather than *n*.

su	(the) water	**sular**	(the) water(s)
suyun	the water's	**suların**	the waters'

3. Possessive suffixes

There is a possessive suffix for each person, singular and plural. That of the third person singular is -(s) V^4; that of the third person plural is -l V^2 r i/ı. These third person possessive suffixes translate (awkwardly) as 'of him,' 'of her,' 'of it,' 'of them.'

The possessive suffixes for all persons are

singular

1st person	-(V^4) m	of me
2nd person	-(V^4) n	of you
3rd person	-(s) V^4	of him, etc.

plural

1st person	-(V^4) m V^4 z	of us
2nd person	-(V^4) n V^4 z	of you
3rd person	-l V^2 r i/ı	of them

NOTE: When an originally Arabic noun with a final 'ayn (see Lesson 6, section 5) receives a third singular possessive suffix, the result may be

camii	mosque of him
(or) *camisi*	mosque of him (This form is more in vogue.)

4. Types I and II possessive constructions

TYPE I

FIRST MEMBER	SECOND MEMBER
çocuğun	*bahçesi*
of the child, the child's	(the) garden of him
i.e., (the) garden of the child	
çocuğun	*bahçeleri*
of the child, the child's	(the) gardens of him
i.e., (the) gardens of the child	
çocukların	*bahçeleri*
of the children, the children's	garden(s) of them
i.e., (the) garden(s) of the children	

Note that this last example is ambiguous. The word *bahçeleri* may be the singular (*bahçe*) plus the third plural possessive suffix (*-leri*) required by the first member (*çocukların*), i.e., *bahçe-leri*. If so, the words *çocukların bahçeleri* mean '(the) garden of the children.' But the word *bahçeleri* may also be the plural (*bahçeler*) plus the third plural possessive suffix (*-leri*) required by the first member (*çocukların*). Two plural suffixes never come on the same noun: hence the logically expectable *bahçe-ler-leri* does not occur. Thus *çocukların bahçeleri* may mean both

> (the) garden of the children
> (the) gardens of the children

The ambiguity may be resolved in one of two ways: the context is left to show whether one or more gardens is intended; a singular possessive suffix is given the second member, even though the first member is plural: *çocukların bahçesi*, '(the) garden of the children,' in which 'garden' is indubitably singular.

TYPE II

FIRST MEMBER	SECOND MEMBER
çocuk	*bahçesi*
child (or) children	(the) garden of him, (the) garden of them
i.e., (the) child-garden, children-garden, kindergarten, children's park, playground	
çocuk	*bahçeleri*
child (or) children	(the) gardens of him, (the) gardens of them
i.e., (the) child-gardens, children-gardens, kindergartens, playgrounds	

63

A comparison of the two types of possessive construction

I.	*çocuğun bahçesi*	(the) garden of the child
II.	*çocuk bahçesi*	(the) child-garden

demonstrates the essential difference in meaning between the two types. That difference turns on the definiteness or indefiniteness of the first member.

In Type I the first member is always definite. Thus the possessive definite suffix, like the objective definite suffix (see Lesson 6, section 2), may be called a sort of definite article in a specialized use. The student should note, however, that by express stipulation the first member of a Type I possessive construction may become indefinite.

	iyi bir çocuğun büyük bir bahçesi	a large garden of a (or one) good child
Compare	*iyi çocuğun büyük bir bahçesi*	a large garden of the good child
and	*iyi çocuğun büyük bahçesi*	(the) large garden of the good child

In a Type II possessive construction the first member is not definite. Instead, as in the possessive construction *çocuk bahçesi*, a singular first member frequently is used collectively or generically—here in the sense of any and all children. This phenomenon, the fact that a singular may have a generic or collective (plural) meaning, is very frequent in Turkish.

Type II serves where English would use an adjective of nationality.

	Türk lisanı	(the) Turkish language
	Türk alfabesi	(the) Turkish alphabet

5. Personal pronouns as members of possessive constructions

A possessive construction whose first member is a personal pronoun is Type I because personal pronouns are definite. The personal pronoun (the first member) need not be expressed unless it is desired to emphasize the possessor's identity.

bahçem	my garden	*benim bahçem*	*my* garden

In informal speech incomplete possessive constructions of the first and second person (possessive suffix omitted) are not infrequent.

	bizim bahçe	our garden (for *bahçemiz*)
	sizin bahçe	your garden (for *bahçeniz*)

6. Possessive complexes

A possessive construction (i.e., the complete construction with all its suffixes) may itself serve as first or second member of another possessive construction. Such a possessive relationship—one or both of whose members may themselves consist of one (or more) possessive constructions—is called a possessive complex.

TYPE I

FIRST MEMBER	SECOND MEMBER
(*benim*) *çocuğumun*	*bahçesi*
(of me) of the child of me	(the) garden of him

i.e., (the) garden of the child of me, (the) garden of my child, my child's garden

The Type I unit (*benim çocuğum*) becomes the first member of the Type I complex. The first member (*çocuğum*) must have a possessive definite suffix: *çocuğumun*.

TYPE II

FIRST MEMBER	SECOND MEMBER
Ankara	*çocuk bahçesi*
of Ankara	(the) kindergarten (of it)

i.e., (the) Ankara Kindergarten or Nursery School (name of an institution)

The Type II unit (*çocuk bahçesi*) becomes the second member of the possessive complex (*Ankara çocuk bahçesi*). The second member of the Type II complex (the unit *çocuk bahçesi*) already has a possessive suffix (*bahçe-si*). No word may bear more than one possessive suffix. Hence the *-si* of *bahçesi* does double duty, serving (a) as possessive suffix for the Type II possessive construction *çocuk bahçesi*, and (b) as possessive suffix for the possessive complex, *Ankara çocuk bahçesi*, '(the) Ankara Kindergarten.'

Compare

Ankaranın	*çocuk bahçesi*
of Ankara	(the) kindergarten of it

i.e., Ankara's kindergarten

Ankaranın	*çocuk bahçeleri*
of Ankara	(the) kindergartens of it

i.e., Ankara's kindergartens

İstanbul Caddesi	Istanbul Avenue
Ankara Bulvarı	Ankara Boulevard
İstanbulun güzel caddeleri	Istanbul's lovely avenues
Ankaranın büyük bulvarları	Ankara's great boulevards

65

Some expressions (mostly place-names) which were originally Type II possessive constructions tend to lose the possessive suffix.

Arnavutköy   Albanian Village (name of a part of Istanbul); older form, *Arnavutköyü*

Other place-names always retain the possessive suffix

Beyoğlu   Bey's-son (name of the downtown section of Istanbul)

In the case of a noun whose absolute form ends in a vowel, note the 'disappearance' of the third person possessive suffix when its possessive form becomes a member of a possessive complex.

yatak odası	bedroom
(benim) yatak odam	my bedroom
(senin) yatak odan	your bedroom
onun yatak odası	his bedroom
(bizim) yatak odamız	our bedroom
(sizin) yatak odanız	your bedroom
onların yatak odası	their bedroom
(benim) yatak odalarım	my bedrooms
(senin) yatak odaların	your bedrooms
onun yatak odaları	his bedrooms
(bizim) yatak odalarımız	our bedrooms
(sizin) yatak odalarınız	your bedrooms
onların yatak odaları	their bedrooms

7. The word *sahip* in possessive constructions

The student should avoid the logical pitfall involved when the word *sahip* (*sahibi* 'owner,' 'possessor,' 'master') is used in possessive constructions. Despite its meaning, this word is not the first member (possessor), but the second member (thing possessed).

A	B	B	A
John's	book	the book	of John
the rug's	owner	the owner	of the rug

Study these examples

1. **halının sahibi**	(the) owner of the rug
2. **halının bir sahibi**	one (an) owner of the rug
3. **bir halının bir sahibi**	an (one) owner of a (one) rug
4. **halıların sahibi**	(the) owner of the rugs
5. **halıların bir sahibi**	an (one) owner of the rugs

66

6. halı sahibi	(the) rug owner
7. bir halı sahibi	a (one) rug owner
8. halı sahipleri	(the) rug owners
9. halının iki sahibi	(the) two owners of the rug
10. iki halı sahibi	(the) two rug owners

8. Suffixes added to a possessive suffix

When other suffixes are added to the possessive suffixes, no phonetic buffer is needed after the possessive suffixes of the first and second persons.

Bahçemi gördüler.	They saw my garden.
Otomobillerimi istediler.	They wanted my cars.
(senin) Kitabını aldılar.	They took your book.
(senin) Kitaplarını okudular.	They read your books.
Paramızı buldular.	They found our money.
Evlerimizi gördüler.	They have seen our houses.
(sizin) Çocuğunuzu gördük.	We saw your child.
(sizin) Çocuklarınızı gördü.	He saw your children.

When other suffixes are added to a third person possessive suffix, singular or plural, a buffer consonant is needed. This buffer—n—is inserted not only when required by an immediately suffixed vowel, but also before a following locative or ablative suffix.

Bahçesini gördüler.	They have seen his garden.
(onun) Bahçelerini gördüler.	They saw his gardens.
Onların bahçesini gördük.	We have seen their garden.
Onların bahçelerini gördük.	We have seen their gardens.

Study the following examples.

1. Babasının evi İstanbulda.	His father's home is in Istanbul.
2. Kız annesine güldü.	The girl laughed at her mother.
3. Senin kitabını bulmadı.	He didn't find your book.
4. Kitabını buldu.	He found his book.
5. Evinde iki çocuk buldular.	They found two children in his house.
6. İki çocuğu senin evinde buldum.	I found the two children in your house.
7. İstanbul şehrinden Ankara şehrine geldi.	He had come from Istanbul (city) to Ankara (city).
8. Onun kız kardeşlerinin evi büyük.	His sisters' house is large.

67

9. Senin kız kardeşlerinin evi büyük.	Your sisters' house is large.
10. Onların kız kardeşlerinin evi büyük.	Their sisters' house is large.
11. Onların babasının evi büyük.	Their father's house is large.
12. Çocuklar annelerine baktılar.	The children looked at their mothers.
13. Kitaplarını bulmadılar.	They didn't find their books.
14. Senin kitaplarını bulmadılar.	They didn't find your books.
15. Parayı evlerinde buldu.	He found the money in their houses (or house).
16. Parayı onların evinde buldu.	He found the money in their house.
17. Parayı Ahmedin ceplerinde buldu.	He found the money in Ahmet's pockets.
18. Parayı senin ceplerinde buldu.	He found the money in your (one person's) pockets.
19. Çocuklarınız dün sabah Ahmedin annesinin evinde iki saat kaldılar.	Yesterday morning your children stayed two hours at Ahmet's mother's house.
20. Küçük oğlunuzun ceplerinde Ahmedin babasının beş lirasını buldum.	I found Ahmed's father's five liras in your little son's pockets.

9. *Kendi*

The word *kendi* 'self' is much used with possessive constructions.

1. to mean 'own' (modifies second member)

kendi kitabım	my own book
kendi kitabın	your own book
kendi kitabı	his (her or its) own book
kendi kitabımız	our own book
kendi kitabınız	your own book
kendi kitapları	their own book or books
kendi kitaplarım	my own books
kendi kitapların	your own books
(onun) kendi kitapları	his own books
kendi kitaplarımız	our own books
kendi kitaplarınız	your own books
onların kendi kitapları	their own books

2. to form the emphatic personal pronoun

(ben) kendim	I myself	(biz) kendimiz
(sen) kendin		(siz) kendiniz
(o) kendisi		(onlar) kendileri

NOTE: *Kendi kendine geldi.*   He came of his own accord.
       Kendine geldi.   He came to (regained consciousness).

Exercises

A. Practice aloud. Translate.

SIMPLE POSSESSIVE CONSTRUCTIONS

1. Ahmedin annesi çok genç.
2. Eviniz nerede?
3. Çocuğun babası geldi.
4. Baban kim?
5. Şehrin suyu çok iyi.
6. Onların babası buraya gelsin!
7. Babaları oraya gitmesinler!
8. Kitabınız bu mu?
9. Halı sahibi parayı aldı.
10. Kimin elması bu?
11. Türk alfabesi kolay.
12. Türk lisanı güç mü?
13. Bahçeniz çok büyük mü?
14. Ankara Bulvarı güzel.
15. Ankaranın bulvarları ne güzel!
16. Yatak odanız küçük mü?
17. Ders odamız sıcak.
18. O kadın otomobil sahibi mi?
19. Ev sahibi nerede?
20. Bu evin sahibi kim?
21. Kendi kitabım evde.
22. Parayı ev sahibi istemedi.
23. Salı günü geldiler.
24. Çay fincanları nerede?
25. Bu ders kitabı çok büyük.

POSSESSIVE COMPLEXES, ETC.

1. Babanızın gözleri güzel.
2. Şehrimizin ağaçları çok büyük.

3. Ahmedin iki oğlu geldiler.
4. Küçük çocuğun annesi çabuk gelsin!
5. Ev sahibinin radyosu çok güzel.
6. Ev sahibiniz nerede?
7. Arkadaşınızın annesinin evi büyük.
8. Kızımın arkadaşları bugün buraya gelmesinler!
9. Kimin babasının evi bu?
10. Oğlunuzun ismi ne?
11. Ev sahiplerinin ismini bilmediler mi?
12. Ahmedin çocuklarına kim baksın?
13. Beyoğlunun caddelerinden geçtim.
14. Kızkardeşimin yatak odasına ne onun kitaplarını
    koydum ne kendi kitaplarımı.
15. Kitaplarımı almadılar mı?
16. Babanızın parasını o çocukların annesine vermeyiniz!
17. Ankara çocuk bahçesinde kimi gördünüz?
18. Oğlumu ve Ahmedin iki kızını görmediniz mi?
19. Benim çocuğumdan bir kitap aldılar.
20. Çanakkaleden Boğaziçine gitti.
21. Beyoğluna ne zaman gittiler?
22. Hiç Toros dağlarını gördünüz mü?
23. Arkadaşının kitabını istemedi.
24. Kendi kitabını istedi.
25. Evime gelme! Arkadaşının evine git!

B. Write in Turkish. Practice aloud.

1. Whom did you find in our classroom?
2. Ahmet's mother went into the boys' bedroom.
3. My brother's landlord put his car into my father's garage.
4. The automobile went from Beyoğlu to Istanbul University.
5. The steamer passed through the Dardanelles.
6. Your little sister's teacups are pretty.
7. My landlord's own house is on Istanbul Street.
8. Your son's feet are large.
9. What is your little brother's name?
10. Why didn't Ahmet's sister go to your sisters' house last night?
11. Have you ever been to Beyoğlu?
12. Ahmet had never seen the Black Sea, but he had seen the Sea of Marmara.
13. They gave my mother's money to the sisters of Mehmet and Erdoğan.

14. He left the small classroom and went into the big one.
15. Istanbul city is very old. Ankara city is new.
16. The new Turkish alphabet is easy.
17. Don't ever go there.
18. The Bosporus is very beautiful. The Dardanelles are beautiful, too.
19. Have you ever seen the Dardanelles?
20. Didn't you go to the Dardanelles yesterday?
21. The car passed through the streets of Beyoğlu. It did not go through Karaköy.
22. Her father's house is in Afyonkarahisar.
23. Is this man a car owner?
24. The owner of the large automobile gave ten liras to the brother of the man who owns that house.
25. Whose books did you take from my friend's father's car?

Lesson 11

Infinitives. General Verbs

---

1. eve girmek

to enter the house, action of entering the house

2. Ahmedin eve girmesi

Ahmet's entering the house, the fact that Ahmet did (has, does, or will) enter the house

3. kızkardeşinizin evimize gelmemesi

the fact that your sister did (has, does, or will) not come to our house

4. Okumayı çok sever.

He greatly likes reading.

5. O kitabı okumadan size verdim.

I gave you that book without having read it.

6. Oraya gitmek çok güç.

Going there is very difficult. It's very difficult to go there.

7. Oraya gitmemiz güç.

It's hard for us to go there.

8. İngilizcede bu söz ne demek?

What does this word mean in English?

9. Onu görmeye geldiler.

They came in order to see him.

10. Gitmek istemedi.

He didn't want to go.

11. Gitmemek istedi.

He wanted not to go.

12. Yüzmek istedi.

He wanted to swim.

13. Yüzmek bilmez.

He doesn't know how to swim.

14. Türkçe bilir misiniz?

Do you know Turkish?

15. İngilizce bilmezler mi?

Don't they know English?

16. Çocuklar şeker severler.

Children like candy.

17. Kedi köpekten korkar.

Cats are afraid of dogs.

18. Postacı günde iki defa gelir.

The mailman comes twice a day.

19. **Çay sever misiniz?**	Do you like tea?
20. **Ben eve gelir gelmez size telefon ettim.**	As soon as I got home I phoned you.

---

1. Infinitives

The common infinitive (see Lesson 5, section 1) seldom has suffixes added to it. The light infinitive—the common infinitive minus its final k—frequently receives suffixes.

LIGHT INFINITIVE

POSITIVE		NEGATIVE	
gelme	coming	*gelmeme*	not coming
gitme	going	*gitmeme*	not going

(*onun*) *gitmesi*	his (her, its) going; the fact that he did, has (gone), does, or will go
(*onun*) *gitmemesi*	his (her, its) not going; the fact that he did, has (gone), does, or will not go
babanızın Ankaraya gitmesi	your father's going to Ankara; the fact that your father did go, has gone, does go, or will go to Ankara
annenizin evimize gelmemesi	your mother's not coming to our house (to us); the fact that your mother didn't, hasn't, doesn't, or won't come to our house

The light infinitive may be used as a modifier.

dolma kalem	fountain pen (*dolmak* 'to fill')

With the ablative suffix, the light infinitive means 'without (doing so and so),' 'without (having done so and so).'

Kitabı dün aldı. Bu sabah onu okumadan bana verdi.	He took the book yesterday. This morning, without having read it, he gave (it) to me.

NOTE: Some grammarians discuss this under the heading of a separate suffix, *-madan/-meden*.

73

The light infinitive is usually used when an infinitive is the object of another verb form.

O okumayı çok sever.   He greatly likes reading (really loves to read).

NOTE: The verbs *istemek* 'wish,' 'want,' 'need' and *bilmek* 'know' frequently take a common infinitive as object.

> *Gitmek istedi.*   He wanted to go.
> *Gelmek bilmedi.*   He never arrived.

The common infinitive, without suffixes, may be the subject of the verb 'to be,' or the subject of a predicate adjective when 'be' is not expressed.

> *Oraya gitmek güç(tür).*   To go there (is) difficult.
> compare *Oraya gitmemiz güç(tür).*   Our going there (is) difficult.

For the syllable in parenthesis (*tür*) see the forms of the verb 'to be,' Lesson 14, section 1.

The English 'to mean' is expressed by the common infinitive *demek* plus the (usually unexpressed present tense of the) verb 'to be.'

> *Bu ne demek(tir)?*   What does this mean? (This [is] to say what?)

İngilizcede girl '*kız*' *demek(tir).* In English 'girl' means *kız*.
The English 'that is to say' is also expressed by *demek*.

> *Demek, bunu bilmediler.*   That is to say, they didn't know this.

The infinitives—common or light—may govern the objective definite suffix, or other appropriate suffixes, on preceding substantives, just as do finite verb forms.

> *Ankaraya gitmemeniz iyi oldu.*   The fact that you didn't go to Ankara turned out to be a good thing.

The common infinitive with the suffix -s i/ı z i/ı n means 'without (doing so and so),' 'without having (done so and so).'

Ahmet, kitabımı okumaksızın   Ahmet went to Ankara without reading
    Ankaraya gitti.   (without having read) my book.

The common infinitive with the following combination of two suffixes—(1) the ablative suffix and (2) the conditional suffix (see Lesson 20, section 4)—means 'rather than (doing so and so).'

Sinemaya gitmektense okumayı   Rather than go to the movies, I
    tercih ettim.   preferred to read.

2. General verbs

The general verb forms express what is always true and hence timeless (aorist). This is the time value of these English verbs.

> Mice like cheese.
> Children will fight.
> The postman comes each day.

POSITIVE

The positive general verb forms are made by adding these suffixes to the verb stem.

	SINGULAR	PLURAL
1st	-(GV) r V^4 m	-(GV) r V^4 z
2nd	-(GV) r s V^4 n	-(GV) r s V^4 n V^4 z
3rd	-(GV) r	-(GV) r l V^2 r

The symbol GV represents the 'general verb form vowel' (general vowel).

  a. A verb whose stem ends in a vowel takes no general vowel.
  b. A monosyllabic verb stem ending in a consonant takes V^2 as the general vowel. This 'rule,' however, has many exceptions. General vowels are sometimes shown in dictionaries thus:

almak (*alır*)	to take
bulmak (*bulur*)	to find
görmek (*görür*)	to see
gelmek (*gelir*)	to come

  c. A polysyllabic verb stem ending in a consonant takes V^4 as the general vowel.

The general verb forms express general validity, and habitual or customary action. Since what is always true will also be true in the future, the general also may be used as a future tense. It may also be used to express an intention on the speaker's part, a promise of sorts.

The positive general forms are

	SINGULAR		PLURAL
1st	**giderim**	I go, always go, will go	**gideriz**
2nd	**gidersin**		**gidersiniz**
3rd	**gider**		**giderler**

The positive interrogative forms are

	SINGULAR	PLURAL
1st	**gider miyim?**	**gider miyiz?**
2nd	**gider misin?**	**gider misiniz?**
3rd	**gider mi?**	**giderler mi?**

In the second person plural, these forms are the most polite of all ways to express a command in Turkish.

Lûtfen, kitabınızı bana verir   Will you please give me your book? (or)
misiniz?   Please give me your book.

NEGATIVE

The negative general verb forms are made by suffixing to the (positive) verb stem these suffixes

	SINGULAR	PLURAL
1st	-m V^2 m	-m V^2 y i/ı z
2nd	-m V^2 z s i/ı n	-m V^2 z s i/ı n i/ı z
3rd	-m V^2 z	-m V^2 z l V^2 r
1st	**gitmem**	**gitmeyiz**
2nd	**gitmezsin**	**gitmezsiniz**
3rd	**gitmez**	**gitmezler**

The negative interrogative general verb forms are

	SINGULAR	PLURAL
1st	**gülmez miyim?**	**gülmez miyiz?**
2nd	**gülmez misin?**	**gülmez misiniz?**
3rd	**gülmez mi?**	**gülmezler mi?**

The third singular positive and negative general verb forms (the general participles, see Lesson 16, section 2) are used, the one immediately following the other, to express the idea of 'as soon as.'

Buraya gelir gelmez parayı alınız.   As soon as you come (get) here, take the money.

Ahmet buraya gelir gelmez parayı alsın.   Let Ahmet take the money as soon as he gets here.

Buraya gelir gelmez parayı aldım.   As soon as I got here, I took the money.

Ahmet buraya gelir gelmez Mehmet parayı aldı.   As soon as Ahmet got here, Mehmet took the money.

NOTE:
ister istemez   want to or not, willy-nilly
İster istemez, gitsin.   Let him go, whether he wants to or not.

Exercises

A. Practice aloud. Translate.

1. **Evimize gelmenizi çok isteriz, efendim. Sizi bekleriz, efendim, bekleriz.**
2. **New York'a gitmek çok para ister.**

3. Selmanın Fahrünnisanın bütün kahve fincanlarını kırması ne fena(dır)!
4. Baba, ben sinemaya giderim.
   Ahmet, ders kitabını okudun mu? Dersin hazır mı?
   Okudum, baba, okudum. İki defa okudum.
   Ne dersin Selma, çocuk bu akşam sinemaya gitsin mi, gitmesin mi?
   Gitsin, Mehmet, gitsin. Neden gitmesin?
   Pekiyi, gitsin. Şimdi git, Ahmet. Amma geç kalma!
   Teşekkür ederim, baba. Sana da teşekkür ederim, anne. Geç kalmam.
5. Bu ne demek, Ahmet? Türkçe dersinde yalnız altı numara aldın. Ne oldu?
   Çalışmadın mı? Çok çok çalış. Zaten, hayatta daima çalışmak lâzım(dır).
   Anladın mı, anlamadın mı? Anladım, baba. Çalışırım. Çok çalışırım.
6. Bir çay içer misiniz, beyefendi?
   Hayır, teşekkür ederim. Ben hiç çay içmem.
   O halde bir kahve olmaz mı, efendim?
   Teşekkür ederim, hanımefendi. Lûtfen, bir kahve verir misiniz?
7. Ahmet Bey, çay içmektense kahve içmeyi tercih etti.
8. Ahmet ders kitabının bir kelimesini anlamaksızın okudu.
9. Yolunuz açık olsun, Ahmet Bey!
10. Mehmet her sabah evimize gelir. Ağabeyisi Erdoğan da gelsin!
11. Otobüslerde paralarımızı biletçilere veririz, biletlerimizi onların ellerinden alırız.
12. Ahmet Bey her sabah kahvaltı yapar, gazeteyi okur ve bürosuna gider.
13. Selma Hanım her sabah kahvaltı yapar, eve bakar ve çarşıya gider.
14. Ahmet Bey öğle yemeğini bir lokantada yer.
15. Çay içer misiniz?
16. Hayır efendim, hiç çay içmem.
17. Selim Bey Fransızca iyi bilir. İstanbul Üniversitesinde üç buçuk sene Fransızca okudu.
18. Ahmet geldi mi, gelmedi mi?
19. Henüz gelmedi. Fakat gelir, efendim, gelir.
20. Bu tren istasyondan saat sekizde kalkar.

B. Write in Turkish. Practice aloud.

1. Will Selma drink a glass of milk?
2. Thank you, madam. Selma never drinks milk. Would you please give her a glass of water?
3. Rather than drinking milk, Selma prefers to drink water.
4. Yesterday morning in the Covered Bazaar Ahmet Bey saw two lovely rugs.

5. He wanted to buy them both.
6. The rug owner asked 2,000 liras for the small one and 5,000 liras for the large.
7. Ahmet Bey said, 'That is very high. I will give 4,500 liras for the two.'
8. Without waiting a single moment, the man said, 'No. I want 7,000 liras for the two of them.'
9. As a result, Ahmet Bey left the Covered Bazaar without having bought the rugs.
10. As soon as he returned home, his wife said, 'Well, did you buy (a) rug?'
11. 'No, I didn't buy (one). The rug man wanted 7,000 liras for two nice rugs. I left the bazaar without buying the rugs,' he said.
12. 'Too bad,' said his wife.
13. 'A pity,' said Ahmet Bey, 'but he wanted 7,000 liras. I found that very expensive.'
14. His wife said, 'But I wanted a new rug!'
15. 'Yes, dear,' Ahmet Bey said. 'I'll try to find a nice rug.'

Lesson 12

Past General Verbs. Future Verbs. Adverbs.

Comparison. Emphatics. The Suffix -ç/c V^2

---

1. 1953 senesinde Ahmet Bey Ankaraya haftada iki defa gider miydi?

In 1953 did Ahmet Bey ordinarily go to Ankara twice a week?

2. 1954 senesinde de oraya haftada iki defa gitmez miydi?

Didn't he also regularly go there twice weekly in 1954?

3. O yazarın kitaplarını çok severdim.

I used to be very fond of that writer's books.

4. Kızımız çok iyi dans eder.

Our daughter dances very well.

5. Oğlum benden uzun(dur).

My son is taller than I am.

6. Selma kızkardeşinden (daha) güzel(dir).

Selma is prettier than her sister.

7. En küçüğü, yani en az büyüğü istediler.

They wanted the very smallest one, i.e., the least large one.

8. Yavaş yavaş öğreneceksiniz.

Step by step, you'll learn.

9. Saçları bir gecede bembeyaz oldu.

Her hair turned snow white over night.

10. Ya siz—siz de gitmiyecek misiniz?

And you, aren't you going to go, either?

11. Bence, Ahmet Bey yarın gelmiyecek. Öbür gün gelecek.

It's my opinion that Ahmet Bey won't come tomorrow. He'll come the day after tomorrow.

12. Çocuğun kaç sene okudu?

How long did your child study?

13. Aman! Senelerce, kardeşim, senelerce!

My goodness! Years and years, my friend, years and years!

14.	Ne dersiniz, beyefendi, çocuklar geç kalacaklar mı, kalmıyacaklar mı?	What's your opinion, sir; will the youngsters be late or not?
15.	Her halde geç kalacaklar. Zaten onlar daima geç kalırlar.	They will probably be late. For that matter, they are always late.

1. Past general verbs

There is a past general verb meaning 'used to (do so and so).' It is formed by adding to the third singular positive general form, the suffixes of the past forms of the verb 'to be' (see Lesson 14, section 1), as follows (the vowel in this suffix is V⁴).

	POSITIVE		NEGATIVE	
singular				
1st	**giderdim**	I used to go	**gitmezdim**	I used not to go
2nd	**giderdin**		**gitmezdin**	
3rd	**giderdi**		**gitmezdi**	
plural				
1st	**giderdik**		**gitmezdik**	
2nd	**giderdiniz**		**gitmezdiniz**	
3rd	**giderlerdi**		**gitmezlerdi**	

	POSITIVE INTERROGATIVE		NEGATIVE INTERROGATIVE	
singular				
1st	**gider miydim?**	Did I used to go?	**gitmez miydim?**	Didn't I used to go?
2nd	**gider miydin?**		**gitmez miydin?**	
3rd	**gider miydi?**		**gitmez miydi?**	
plural				
1st	**gider miydik?**		**gitmez miydik?**	
2nd	**gider miydiniz?**		**gitmez miydiniz?**	
3rd	**giderler miydi?**		**gitmezler miydi?**	

2. Future verbs

The future verb forms express a definite intention which the speaker holds as of the time he speaks. As a promise it is more forceful than the general tense.

The suffixes of the positive future verb forms are

	SINGULAR	PLURAL
1st	-(y) V^2 c V^2 ğ i/ı m	-(y) V^2 c V^2 ğ i/ı z
2nd	-(y) V^2 c V^2 k s i/ı n	-(y) V^2 c V^2 k s i/ı n i/ı z
3rd	-(y) V^2 c V^2 k (t i/ı r)	-(y) V^2 c V^2 k l V^2 r (d i/ı r)

When the syllable -t/d i/ı r (see Lesson 14, section 1) is added to the third person singular or plural, the force of the assertion is somewhat strengthened.

Verb stems which end in *e* or *a* change the final *e* to *i* and the final *a* to *ı* before the immediately following (buffer) *y* of the future suffixes.

	SINGULAR		PLURAL
1st	gideceğim	I shall go. I am going to go.	gideceğiz
2nd	gideceksin		gideceksiniz
3rd	gidecek(tir)		gidecekler(dir)
1st	bulacağım	I shall find (it).	bulacağız
2nd	bulacaksın		bulacaksınız
3rd	bulacak(tır)		bulacaklar(dır)
1st	anlıyacağım	I shall understand (it).	anlıyacağız
2nd	anlıyacaksın		anlıyacaksınız
3rd	anlıyacak(tır)		anlıyacaklar(dır)

Note that before the immediately following (buffer) *y* of the future suffixes, a final vowel V^2 becomes the variable vowel *i/ı*.

The future interrogative forms are

	SINGULAR		PLURAL
1st	gidecek miyim?	Shall I go? Am I going to go?	gidecek miyiz?
2nd	gidecek misin?		gidecek misiniz?
3rd	gidecek mi(dir)?		gidecekler mi(dir)?
1st	bulacak mıyım?	Shall I find (it)?	bulacak mıyız?
2nd	bulacak mısın?		bulacak mısınız?
3rd	bulacak mı(dır)?		bulacaklar mı(dır)?
1st	anlıyacak mıyım?	Shall I understand (it)?	anlıyacak mıyız?
2nd	anlıyacak mısın?		anlıyacak mısınız?
3rd	anlıyacak mı(dır)?		anlıyacaklar mı(dır)?

81

The future negative forms are

	SINGULAR		PLURAL
1st	gitmiyeceğim	I shall not go. I am not going to go.	gitmiyeceğiz
2nd	gitmiyeceksin		gitmiyeceksiniz
3rd	gitmiyecek(tir)		gitmiyecekler(dir)
1st	bulmıyacağım	I shall not find (it).	bulmıyacağız
2nd	bulmıyacaksın		bulmıyacaksınız
3rd	bulmıyacak(tır)		bulmıyacaklar(dır)
1st	anlamıyacağım	I shall not understand (it).	anlamıyacağız
2nd	anlamıyacaksın		anlamıyacaksınız
3rd	anlamıyacak(tır)		anlamıyacaklar(dır)

The future negative interrogative verb forms are

	SINGULAR		PLURAL
1st	gitmiyecek miyim?	Am I not going to go?	gitmiyecek miyiz?
2nd	gitmiyecek misin?		gitmiyecek misiniz?
3rd	gitmiyecek mi(dir)?		gitmiyecekler mi(dir)?
1st	bulmıyacak mıyım?	Am I not going to find (it)?	bulmıyacak mıyız?
2nd	bulmıyacak mısın?		bulmıyacak mısınız?
3rd	bulmıyacak mı(dır)?		bulmıyacaklar mı(dır)?
1st	anlamıyacak mıyım?	Am I not going to understand (it)?	anlamıyacak mıyız?
2nd	anlamıyacak mısın?		anlamıyacak mısınız?
3rd	anlamıyacak mı(dır)?		anlamıyacaklar mı(dır)?

3. Adverbs

The same word may serve as adjective and adverb.

iyi bir kız	a good girl
iyi anlamak	to understand well

4. Comparison

The simple expression of comparison requires only the ablative suffix.

benden büyük	bigger than I
sizden iyi	better than you
ondan az	less than that

The fuller expression of comparison adds the adverbs *daha* 'more' or *az* 'less.' The superlative uses the adverbs *en* 'most' or *en az* 'least.'

benden daha büyük	bigger than I
sizden daha iyi	better than you
en büyük	the biggest
en az	the least
sizden az çalışkan	less industrious than you
en az çalışkan	the least industrious

5. Emphatics

Many adjectives have special emphatic forms. Such forms are shown in dictionaries as separate words.

ADJECTIVE		EMPHATIC FORM	
beyaz	white	**bembeyaz**	white as can be, as snow
açık	open	**apaçık**	wide open
uzun	long	**upuzun**	extremely long
çıplak	naked	**çırçıplak**	stark naked
siyah	black	**simsiyah**	jet black

Apart from these emphatics, the ordinary means for securing emphasis is simply to say a word twice.

yavaş	slowly
yavaş yavaş	very slowly
Güldü güldü.	He laughed and laughed.

6. The suffix -ç/c V²

Among the uses of this suffix are
   a. to mean 'as for.'

bence	as for me, as I see it
fikrimce	as for my idea, in my view, etc.

   b. to mean 'ish' (frequently pejorative), '-ly.'

çocukça	like a child, childishly, kiddish, kiddishly
aptalca	stupidly
türkçe	in the Turkish way, i.e., the Turkish language (and so with all languages, *Arapça, Fransızca, Rusça, İngilizce*, etc.)

NOTE: *bu* 'this' forms *bunca* 'thus,' 'in this way,' 'this much.'

c.	*yüzlerce*	hundreds and hundreds, hundred after hundred
	yıllarca	years and years, year after year

Exercises

A. Practice aloud. Translate.

1. Evim evinizden daha büyük(tür).
2. Saidin Amerikadan gelmesi iyi mi olacak?
   Sait henüz Amerikadan gelmedi. O Haziran ayında gelecektir.
3. O yıl, ayda bir Ankaraya giderdik.
4. Tuzu bana verir misiniz, lûtfen?
5. Ne dersiniz, efendim; oraya gidecek miyiz, gitmiyecek miyiz?
6. Size geldiler mi?
   Evet efendim, iki defa geldiler.
   İki defa mı? O halde, bize de gelecekler.
   Her halde gelecekler.
7. Ahmet Beylere gitmediniz mi?
   Gitmedim. Zaten, ben oraya hiç gitmem.
8. Gazeteyi açar açmaz bunu gördüm.
9. İki çocuk koşmaya başladılar.
10. Kızın saçları simsiyah.
11. Çok kitap okumak iyi.
12. Küçük kızın okuması iyi.
13. Bu yazıları kim yazdı?
    Ben yazdım.
    Çocuğum, böyle yazma! Daha iyi yazmak lâzım!
14. En güzel elmalar kimin (elmaları)?
15. Bunlar sizin mi?
16. Babam saat 7:00de kalkar, kahvaltı yapar, gazeteyi okur, saat 8:30da
    otomobile biner, bürosuna gider.
17. Okumak istemez mi?
    Hiç istemez.
18. Siz bugün gitmiyecek misiniz?
19. Hayır, fakat yarın gideceğim.
20. Bunları kime vereceksiniz?
21. Ahmet, parayı bana vermeden İtalyaya gitmiyecek.
22. Fikrinizce, Ahmet paramı alır mı?
23. Ahmet annenizin evine yarın gitsin mi, gitmesin mi?
24. Dün gelmediler fakat yarın gelecekler.
25. Parayı bize verecek misiniz, vermiyecek misiniz?

B. Write in Turkish. Practice aloud.

1. Why aren't you going to go to Beyoğlu?

2. From whom did Selma's father buy his car?
3. In which garage will he put it?
4. Which movie are they going to go to?
5. Mehmet never goes to the movies.
6. We used to go to the movies twice a week.
7. As I see it, your son's not having read this book is (a) bad (thing).
8. They searched for days and days but they did not find the dog.
9. For whom did you wait?
10. I shall expect you at my house tomorrow.
11. As soon as I got to Ankara, I phoned Mehmet Bey.
12. He will not go to Ankara without (first) giving you the books.
13. My dog is bigger than Selma's dog.
14. His dog is completely white but my dog is jet black.
15. Go slow!
16. I didn't entirely understand.
17. The smallest girl ate the biggest apple.
18. Is Ahmet going to come, or not?
19. In Ahmet's opinion, should Selma come, or not?
20. Why don't you work harder?

Lesson 13

Postpositions. Expressions of Location

1. **Ahmet ile Mehmet beraber geldiler.** — Ahmet and Mehmet came together.
2. **Ahmet ile Mehmet geldiler.** — Ahmet and (with) Mehmet came.
3. **Ahmetle Mehmet geldiler.** — Ahmet and (with) Mehmet came.
4. **Kalemim ile yazma!** — Don't write with my pencil!
5. **Kalemimle yazma!** — Don't write with my pencil!
6. **Bunun ile yazın!** — Write with this (one)!
7. **Bununla yaz!** — Write with this!
8. **Saat ondan evvel gelmiyecekler.** — They won't come before ten o'clock.
9. **Otomobil bana doğru geldi.** — The car came straight at me.
10. **Babası gibi, çocuk okumayı hiç sevmez.** — (Just) like his father, the child doesn't like studying at all.
11. **Sizin gibi bir adam hiç gördüler mi?** — Have they ever seen a man like you?
12. **Kitap büyük kutunun altında (dır).** — The book is under the big box.
13. **Kitabı kutunun altından alınız.** — Take the book from under the box.
14. **Kitabı kutunun arkasında buldunuz mu?** — Did you find the book behind the box?
15. **Kitabı kutunun altına koyacaklar mı?** — Will they put the book under the box?
16. **Kitaplarınızı kutunun içinde gördük.** — We saw your books inside the box.

1. Postpositions

Turkish postpositions—some of them suffixes, some of them independent words—follow substantives and govern them much as English prepositions govern the substantives which they precede.

Classified according to the suffixes which they require on the preceding substantives, Turkish postpositions are:

CLASS I: postpositions which require that the preceding substantive have the ablative suffix;

CLASS II: postpositions which require that the preceding substantive have the dative suffix; and

CLASS III: postpositions that require a preceding personal or interrogative pronoun or singular demonstrative pronoun to have the possessive suffix but that require no suffix on other preceding substantives.

The important postpositions include

CLASS I (ablative suffix on preceding substantive)
başka—other than, apart from, except for

benden başka	except for me
kitaplarımdan başka	apart from my books

Başka may also be an adjective.

başka bir kitap	another book
Contrast: *diğer kitap*	(the) other book

evvel—before (in time)

bizden evvel	before us, earlier than we
ondan evvel	before ten (before him, etc.)
saat ondan evvel	before ten o'clock

sonra—after

onlardan sonra	after them
saat altıdan sonra	after six o'clock
altı saatten sonra	after six hours

beri—subsequent to, since

on saatten beri	for (the) past ten hours
saat ondan beri	since ten o'clock
bin sekiz yüz altmış üçten beri	since 1863

dolayı—because of

sizden dolayı	because of you
parasından dolayı	because of his money

CLASS II (dative suffix on preceding substantive)

kadar—up to, until, as far as

saat ona kadar	until ten o'clock
evime kadar	as far as my house

Kadar may also be a noun meaning 'amount.'

bu kadar	this much
ne kadar?	how much?

doğru—straight toward

bana doğru	right at me
evine doğru	straight toward his house

Doğru may also be a modifier meaning 'right,' 'true,' 'straight.'

doğru sözler	true words

karşı—against, opposite, anti-

bana karşı	against me
çocuklara karşı	against (the) children

göre—according to

onlara göre	according to them
gazeteye göre	according to the newspaper

rağmen—despite

ona rağmen	despite that
parasına rağmen	in spite of his money

nazaran—compared with, in regard to

İzmire nazaran Ankara daha büyük(tür).	Compared with Izmir, Ankara is larger.

CLASS III (no suffix on any preceding substantive except a personal pronoun, a singular interrogative pronoun, and a singular demonstrative pronoun—these require the possessive suffix)

ile—'with,' independent word, also used in the suffixed form -l V^2. After a final vowel, suffixed -l V^2 may become -y l V^2. Both *ile* and -(y) l V^2 frequently are followed by *beraber*, 'together': *ile beraber* or -(y) l V^2 *beraber*, 'together with.'

benim ile, benimle	with me
çocuk ile, çocukla	with (the) child
bunun ile beraber, bununla beraber	together with this, moreover
kitabı ile, kitabıyla	with his book
annesi ile, annesiyle	with his mother

NOTE: *İle* is frequently used to mean 'and': *Ahmet ile Mehmet*, 'Ahmet and Mehmet.'

gibi—like, similar to

sizin gibi	like you
bunun gibi	like this
babası gibi	like his father

için—for, for the purpose of, because of

benim için	for me, because of me
bunun için	for this, because of this
çocuklar için	for (the) children
anlamak için	for understanding

NOTE: niçin (from *ne için*) for what? why?

üzere (or) *üzre*—upon

bunun üzerine	upon this, thereupon
gitmek üzere	on the point of going, in order to go, on condition of going

2. Expressions of location

Much of the work of English prepositions is done in Turkish by nouns of place used in possessive constructions.

üst—top, upper part

kutunun üstüne	toward the top of the box
kutunun üstünde	on (the) top of the box
kutunun üstünden	from the top of the box
Kitabım kutunun üstünde(dir).	My book (is) on top of the box.
Kitabımı kutunun üstüne koydular.	They put my book on top of the box.

Üst may also be an adjective.

üst kat	top floor, top story

alt—bottom, lower part

Para o kitabın altında(dır).	The money (is) under that book.
Paranızı o kitabın altına koydu.	He put your money under that box.
Parayı o kitabın altından almadınız mı?	Didn't you take the money from under that book?

Alt may also be an adjective.

alt taraf	bottom side

89

yan—side, (the) space or place next

Yanınızda iki çocuk gördüm.	I saw two children beside you.
Yanıma gel!	Come here to me!
O köpek, sahibinin *yanından hiç ayrılmaz.*	That dog never goes away from his master's side.

Yan may also be an adjective.

yan kapı	side door

ara—midst, space between

Aramızda, böyle bir şey *hiç olmaz.*	Between us, nothing of the sort will happen at all.
Kalemimi iki kitabın *arasına koydum.*	I put my pencil between the two books.
At, iki otomobilin *arasından geçti.*	The horse went (passed) between the two cars.

Note this pattern:

Ankara ile İstanbul arasında	between Ankara and Istanbul
kız ile babesinin arasında	between the girl and her father

Ara may also be an adjective.

ara kapı	middle door

iç—(the) inside

Kutunun içinde ne buldunuz?	What did you find in (inside) the box?
Kitaplarımı büyük kutunun *içine koydular.*	They put my books into the big box.

İç may also be an adjective.

iç kapı	inside door

dış—(the) outside

Evi şehrin dışında(dır).	His house (is) outside the city.

Dış may also be an adjective.

dış kapı	outside door

üzere or *üzre*—the place or space over

Evinizin üzerinde büyük *bir kuş gördüm.*	I saw a big bird over your house.
Evin üzerinden iki uçak *geçti.*	Two planes passed over the house.

arka—back part, space in back

Evinizin arkasında kimi *gördüm?*	Whom did I see behind your house?

90

Kutunun arkasına bir kitap koydu.	He put a book behind the box.
Çocuklar arkamdan geçtiler.	The children passed behind me.

Arka may also be an adjective.

arka kapı	back door

ön—front part, space in front

Evinizin önünde ne oldu?	What happened in front of your house?
Kitapları kutunun önüne koyma!	Don't put the books in front of the box!
Önümüzden iki otomobil geçti.	Two cars passed (crossed) in front of us.

Ön may also be an adjective.

ön kapı	front door

Also note:

yukarı	up, space that is higher, upstairs
aşağı	opposite of *yukarı*
dışarı	outside, space that is out
içeri	opposite of *dışarı*

Exercises

A. Practice aloud. Translate.

1. Arkamızdan kim geçti?
2. Önümüzden geçmiyecekler mi?
3. Sizden sonra kim geldi?
4. Sizden dolayı, kardeşiniz de geç geldi.
5. Niçin bana bunun gibi bir elma vermedin?
6. Kutunun içinde ne buldunuz?
7. Gazeteyi cebinden aldı.
8. Evi dağın üstünde(dir).
9. Köpek sahibinin sesini bilir.
10. Benim için çay getirdiler.
11. Niçin saat sekizden evvel geldiler?
12. Çocuk babasının kalemiyle yazdı.
13. Niçin çalıştın?
14. Anlamak için, öğrenmek için çalıştık.
15. Bunun gibi bir kitap hiç okumadım.

B. Write in Turkish. Practice aloud.

1. What did Ahmet put in his pocket?
2. Where did Selma find the teacups?
3. She found one cup in the box (and) the others behind it.
4. Who took my book?
5. Ahmet did.
6. Where did he put it?
7. He put it beside the tree.
8. Where's Nilüfer?
9. She's gone to the movies.
10. Did she go alone?
11. She did not.
12. With whom did she go?
13. She went with Ahmet's sister.
14. Will they be late?
15. No. They'll come here before 9:30.

Lesson 14

The Verb 'to Be.' *Var* and *Yok*.

The Resumptive Question

---

1. **Ahmet gençtir, değil mi?**	Ahmet is young, isn't he?
2. **Onlar genç idiler.**	They were young.
3. **Onlar gençtiler, değil mi?**	They were young, weren't they?
4. **Siz Türk müsünüz, efendim?**	Are you a Turk, sir?
5. **Evet, efendim, Türküm.**	Yes, sir, I am Turkish.
6. **Annesi Fransız değil miydi?**	Wasn't his mother French?
7. **Annesinin kaç evi vardır?**	How many houses does his mother have?
8. **Bundan bir kaç sene evvel annesinin üç evi vardı, fakat bugün hiç bir evi yoktur.**	A few years ago his mother owned three houses but today she has none at all.
9. **Babasının parası yok muydu?**	Didn't her father have money?
10. **Vardı.**	He did.
11. **Kitabım burada değil(dir).**	My book is not here.
12. **Selmanın kitabı yok(tur).**	Selma doesn't have a book.

---

1. The verb 'to be'

The Turkish verb 'to be' is defective. It lacks the infinitive and several tenses. These missing forms may be replaced by corresponding forms of *olmak* 'to become.'

Some forms of 'to be' are suffixes. This is true of the present forms.

	SINGULAR	PLURAL
1st person	-(y) V^4 m	-(y) V^4 z
2nd person	-s V^4 n	-s V^4 n V^4 z
3rd person	-t/d V^4 r	-t/d V^4 r l V^2 r

NOTE: The third singular and plural are frequently omitted. (See Lesson 3, section 3.)

The indefinite article (*bir*) is not used

a. with negative of 'to be'

$\quad\quad\quad\quad$ *Çocuk değilim.* $\quad\quad$ I'm not a child.

b. with expressions of occupation, nationality, etc.

$\quad\quad\quad\quad$ *Amerikalıyım.* $\quad\quad$ I am an American.

The generic is frequently used where English expects a plural.

$\quad\quad\quad\quad$ *Talebeyiz.* $\quad\quad$ We are students.

PRESENT POSITIVE

singular

1st	**Gençim.**	I am young.	**Talebeyim.**	I am a student.
2nd	**Gençsin.**		**Talebesin.**	
3rd	**Gençtir.**		**Talebedir.**	

plural

1st	**Gençiz.**		**Talebeyiz.**
2nd	**Gençsiniz.**		**Talebesiniz.**
3rd	**Gençtirler.**		**Talebedirler.**

PRESENT INTERROGATIVE

singular

1st	**Genç miyim?**	**Talebe miyim?**
2nd	**Genç misin?**	**Talebe misin?**
3rd	**Genç midir?**	**Talebe midir?**

plural

1st	**Genç miyiz?**	**Talebe miyiz?**
2nd	**Genç misiniz?**	**Talebe misiniz?**
3rd	**Genç midirler?**	**Talebe midirler?**

In the past, the verb 'to be' has two sets of forms: those that are suffixes and those that are independent words. Their meanings are identical.

	ENCLITIC FORM	INDEPENDENT FORM	
singular			
1st	-t/d V^4 m	idim	I was
2nd	-t/d V^4 n	idin	you were
3rd	-t/d V^4	idi	he, she, it was
plural			
1st	-t/d V^4 k	idik	we were
2nd	-t/d V^4 n V^4 z	idiniz	you were
3rd	-t/d V^4 l V^2 r	idiler	they were

PAST POSITIVE

singular

1st	Gençtim.	Genç idim.
2nd	Gençtin.	Genç idin.
3rd	Gençti.	Genç idi.

plural

1st	Gençtik.	Genç idik.
2nd	Gençtiniz.	Genç idiniz.
3rd	Gençtiler.	Genç idiler.

In the case of a substantive ending in a vowel (e.g., *talebe* 'student'), a *y* is inserted between the final vowel and the past suffixes.

singular

1st	Talebeydim.	Talebe idim.
2nd	Talebeydin.	Talebe idin.
3rd	Talebeydi.	Talebe idi.

plural

1st	Talebeydik.	Talebe idik.
2nd	Talebeydiniz.	Talebe idiniz.
3rd	Talebeydiler.	Talebe idiler.

A *y* is also inserted between the interrogative syllable and the past suffixed forms.

Genç miydiler?

With 'to be,' the negative is always *değil* 'not.'

	PRESENT NEGATIVE	PAST NEGATIVE		
singular				
1st	Genç değilim.	Genç değildim.	or	değil idim.
2nd	Genç değilsin.	Genç değildin.		değil idin.
3rd	Genç değildir.	Genç değildi.		değil idi.

95

plural

			or	
1st	Genç değiliz.	Genç değildik.	or	değil idik.
2nd	Genç değilsiniz.	Genç değildiniz.		değil idiniz.
3rd	Genç değildirler.	Genç değildiler.		değil idiler.

PRESENT NEGATIVE INTERROGATIVE   PAST NEGATIVE INTERROGATIVE

singular

			or	
1st	Genç değil miyim?	Genç değil miydim?	or	değil mi idim?
2nd	Genç değil misin?	Genç değil miydin?		değil mi idin?
3rd	Genç değil midir?	Genç değil miydi?		değil mi idi?

plural

			or	
1st	Genç değil miyiz?	Genç değil miydik?	or	değil mi idik?
2nd	Genç değil misiniz?	Genç değil miydiniz?		değil mi idiniz?
3rd	Genç değil midirler?	Genç değil miydiler?		değil mi idiler?

2. *Var* and *yok*

The two words *var* 'extant,' 'in existence' and *yok* 'non-extant,' 'not in existence' are of remarkable frequence and importance in Turkish.

Their principal functions are to express: possession, the verb 'to have' and the English 'there is' and 'there are.'

Var and *yok* are always used with some form of the verb 'to be'—understood if not expressed. In the third present, singular and plural, the verb form is usually not expressed.

Bir çocuğum var(dır).	I have a child.
Çocuğun var mı(dır)?	Have you a child?
Ahmedin iki çocuğu var(dır).	Ahmet has two children.
İki çocuğumuz var(dır).	We have two children.
Çocuğunuz var mı(dır)?	Do you have children?
Onların bir çocukları var(dır).	They have one child.
Çocuğum yok(tur).	I have no children.
Çocuğu yok mu(dur)?	Doesn't he have a child?
Bir çocuğum vardı (var idi).	I had a child.
Ahmedin bir çocuğu yok muydu?	Didn't Ahmet have a child?
Evde ne var(dır)?	What is there in the house?
Evde beş kutu var(dır).	There are five boxes in the house.
Evde ne vardı?	What was there in the house?
Evde beş kutu vardı.	There were five boxes in the house.
Sizde para var mı(dır)?	Do you have any money ('on you')?

96

Sizde para yok mu(dur)?	Don't you have any money with you?
Ahmette hiç para yoktu (yok idi).	Ahmet didn't have any money with him.
Mehmette çok para vardı (var idi).	Mehmet had a lot of money with him.
Mehmedin çok parası vardı (var idi).	Mehmet was very rich (had a lot of money).

3. The resumptive question

In English one repeats a verb in the interrogative in order to gather up the conversation and proceed. In Turkish, the same effect is produced, for any verb, simply by adding *değil mi?* (compare French 'n'est-ce pas?').

Gitti, değil mi?	He went, didn't he?
Gelmiyecekler, değil mi?	They won't come, will they?

Exercises

A. Practice aloud. Translate.

1. Otomobiliniz nerede, Ahmet Bey?
2. Otomobilim yok, efendim. Vardı fakat onu sattım.
3. Otomobiliniz iyi miydi, Ahmet Bey?
4. İyi değildi. Çok eskiydi. Onun için sattım.
5. Küçük Selma nerede, Mihri Hanım?
6. Burada değildir. Selmayı bugün görmedim.
7. Fakat bugün buraya gelecek, değil mi?
8. Evet, Mihri Hanım, inşallah gelecek.
9. Dün öğleden sonra evinizde kim vardı?
10. Mehmet vardı. Ahmet vardı. Bir kaç arkadaş geldiler. Oturduk, konuştuk. O kadar ...
11. İki kızkardeşiniz var, değil mi?
12. Hayır, yalnız bir kızkardeşim var, fakat kocamın iki kızkardeşi var.
13. Türkiyede elma var mı?
14. Evet, hem de çok elma var.
15. Bahçenizde iki elma ağacı var, değil mi?

B. Write in Turkish. Practice aloud.

1. Whose book is this?
2. Who doesn't have a book?

3. These are yours, aren't they?
4. These aren't yours, are they?
5. She had four sisters, didn't she?
6. Your book is at my house.
7. There are no books in their house.
8. Ahmet's father has two automobiles.
9. Your father didn't have an automobile, did he?
10. Is Ahmet there?

Lesson 15

The Suffixes -l V⁴, -s V⁴ z, and -l V⁴ k.

Past Indefinite, Past Narrative,

and Past Perfect Verb Forms

1. **Yaşlı kadın ölmüş.** | The aged woman (reportedly) has died (died, is dead).
2. **Yaşlı kadın ölmüştür.** | The aged woman died. (narrative)
3. **Yaşlı kadın ölmüştü.** | The aged woman had died.
   (*Yaşlı kadın ölmüş idi.*)
4. **Bugün hava yağmurludur.** | Today the weather is rainy.
5. **Siz Ankaralı mısınız?** | Are you from Ankara?
   Evet, Ankaralıyım. | Yes, I am from Ankara.
6. **Ahmet gitmiş mi?** | Has Ahmet gone (so far as you know)?

   Her halde gitmiş. | Certainly he seems to have gone.
7. **Ha! Ben onunla beraber gitmişim! Öyle mi?** | So! I'm supposed to have gone with him! (I allegedly went with him!) Is that how it is?

8. **Bir varmış, bir yokmuş. Allahın kulu çokmuş ...** | Once upon a time ... (Once there was, once there wasn't, they say: but God's slaves are many ...)

9. **Radyonuz kaç lambalı?** | How many tubes does your radio have?

10. **Eski ev elektrikli mi, elektriksiz mi?** | Does the old house have electricity or not?

1. The suffix -l V^4

The suffix -l V^4 (whose meaning is the opposite of -s V^4 z, see section 2, below) forms adjectives meaning 'having,' 'possessed of.'

para	money	*paralı*	rich
ev	house	*evli*	married (has a home)
elektrik	electricity	*elektrikli*	electrified, wired for electricity
yaş	age (of a human)	*yaşlı*	aged

2. The suffix -s V^4 z

This suffix, the opposite of the suffix -l V^4, forms adjectives meaning 'without,' 'deprived of,' '-less.'

parasız	moneyless	*tuzsuz*	salt free
susuz	waterless, thirsty	*şekersiz*	without sugar

3. The suffix -l V^4 k

This suffix forms nouns, usually abstract.

evli	married	*evlilik*	matrimony
öğretmen	teacher	*öğretmenlik*	profession of being a teacher
büyük	large	*büyüklük*	largeness, size; adulthood; greatness
göz	eye	*gözlük*	eyepiece, glasses
parasız	moneyless	*parasızlık*	poverty
susuz	arid	*susuzluk*	waterlessness, thirst

Note also:

satılık ev	house for sale
kiralık ev	house for rent
şimdilik	for the present, for now
beş kişilik otomobil	five-passenger car
günlük gazete	daily newspaper

4. Past indefinite verb forms

Turkish seldom expresses past time without simultaneously specifying one aspect of what happened, which English usually ignores. This aspect is the definiteness of the speaker's (or writer's) knowledge of what happened.

The word *gitti* (past definite) means 'He (definitely) went.' The corresponding past indefinite form means 'He (apparently, allegedly, reportedly, presumably, or ostensibly) went (*but* I am not sure enough of this assertion to be able honestly to say *gitti*).'

The past indefinite verb forms use these suffixes

	SINGULAR	PLURAL
1st	-m V^4 ş V^4 m	-m V^4 ş V^4 z
2nd	-m V^4 ş s V^4 n	-m V^4 ş s V^4 n V^4 z
3rd	-m V^4 ş	-m V^4 ş l V^2 r

	POSITIVE		NEGATIVE
singular			
1st	Gitmişim.	I (allegedly) went, did go, have gone.	Gitmemişim.
2nd	Gitmişsin.	You (reportedly) went, did go, have gone.	Gitmemişsin.
3rd	Gitmiş.		Gitmemiş.
plural			
1st	Gitmişiz.		Gitmemişiz.
2nd	Gitmişsiniz.		Gitmemişsiniz.
3rd	Gitmişler.		Gitmemişler.

	INTERROGATIVE	NEGATIVE INTERROGATIVE
singular		
1st	Gitmiş miyim?	Gitmemiş miyim?
2nd	Gitmiş misin?	Gitmemiş misin?
3rd	Gitmiş mi?	Gitmemiş mi?
plural		
1st	Gitmiş miyiz?	Gitmemiş miyiz?
2nd	Gitmiş misiniz?	Gitmemiş misiniz?
3rd	Gitmişler mi?	Gitmemişler mi?

5. Past narrative verb forms

The preceding verb forms—past indefinite—with the addition of only a final -t/d V^4 r to the third singular and plural, provide a past narrative tense much used by newspapers and storytellers.

The past narrative verb forms (third person) are

	POSITIVE		NEGATIVE	
singular				
3rd	*Gitmiştir.*	He went.	*Gitmemiştir.*	He did not go.

plural

   3rd *Gitmişlerdir.*   *Gitmemişlerdir.*

singular

   3rd *Gitmiş midir?*   *Gitmemiş midir?*

plural

   3rd *Gitmiş midirler?*   *Gitmemiş midirler?*

6. Past perfect verb forms

Combining the verb form ending in -m V⁴ ş (the past participle; see Lesson 16, section 2) with the past of the verb 'to be' produces a verb form whose tense value is well back in the past. According to context it may be understood as past ('I went') or, frequently, as past perfect ('I had gone'). The past perfect verb forms are

	POSITIVE		NEGATIVE	
singular				
1st	**Gitmiştim.**	I had gone.	**Gitmemiştim.**	I had not gone.
2nd	**Gitmiştin.**		**Gitmemiştin.**	
3rd	**Gitmişti.**		**Gitmemişti.**	
plural				
1st	**Gitmiştik.**		**Gitmemiştik.**	
2nd	**Gitmiştiniz.**		**Gitmemiştiniz.**	
3rd	**Gitmişlerdi.**		**Gitmemişlerdi.**	

INTERROGATIVE	NEGATIVE INTERROGATIVE
Gitmiş miydim? etc.	*Gitmemiş miydim?* etc.

In addition, the independent forms of the past verb 'to be' may be used.

POSITIVE		NEGATIVE	
Bulmuş idim.	I had found.	*Bulmamış idim.*	I had not found.
etc.		etc.	

Negative forms may use the word *değil*.

       Gitmiş değildim. (or *Gitmemiştim.*)   I had not gone.
       etc.

Exercises

A. Practice aloud. Translate.

  1. **Kardeşinizin yatak odası yukarıda mı, aşağıda mı?**
  2. **Kızkardeşimizi gördünüz mü?**
  3. **Parayı kutunun altından kim aldı?**

4. **Ahmet dün sabah buraya gelmiş, bunu demiş, şunu demiş, sonra kız-kardeşimin parasını almış ve gitmiştir.** (The final *-tir* serves for all verbs. See above section 5.)
5. **Ahmede göre, onlar buraya gelmezler.**
6. **Tramvayın ön tarafında iki yer bulduk.**
7. **Çocuğum, bugün içeriye girme!**
8. **1937 senesinden evvel İstanbula gitmemiş miydi?**
9. **Su, ağzına kadar çıktı.**
10. **Sana göre, kızkardeşim Ahmedin otomobiline binmedi.**
11. **Ondan başka, ne istediler?**
12. **Niçin gelmiyecekler?**
13. **Buraya pek gelmek istemiyecekler.**
14. **Çay fincanlarının içlerine ne koydu?**
15. **Tren, istasyonda beş dakika kaldı.**
16. **Siz çoktan beri Türkiyeye gitmediniz.**
17. **Eviniz bahçeli mi(dir)?**
18. **Bundan beş gün evvel çocuklar seyahate çıktılar.**
19. **Bu ev satılık mı(dır), kiralık mı(dır)?**
20. **İstanbulun günlük gazeteleri çok.**
21. **Fakirliğime rağmen, ben o adamdan para almam!**
22. **Ahmet ve Erdoğan İstanbula gitmek için çok çalışmışlar.**
23. **Büyük kutu yanınızda kalsın mı?**
    Evet, bir iki hafta kadar kalsın.
24. **Trenin önünden geçme!**
25. **Çocuklar, dış kapıyı açmayınız, lûtfen!**

B. Write in Turkish. Practice aloud.

1. Mehmet, has Ahmet gone to Istanbul?
   I didn't see him. But he certainly seems to have gone.
   Erdoğan, did you see Ahmet?
   I did, sir. He didn't go to Istanbul; he went to Edirne.
2. Do you want your coffee with or without sugar?
3. I like tea with lemon.
4. This café au lait is very good.
5. Had Ahmet's brother died before 1955?
6. In 1949 I had two houses. Now I have three. (There are three of them.)
7. At that time you weren't married, were you?
8. My father always desired goodness, rightness, and beauty.
9. According to Ahmet, he hasn't gone.
10. According to Ahmet, he hadn't gone.

Lesson 16

The Partitive. Participles. Gerund in -t/d V^4 k.

Indirect Discourse. Relative Gerundive and Adverb

1. **Kitaplarınızdan hangisini aldılar?**	Which (one) of your books did they take?
2. **Kitaplarınızdan hangilerini istedi?**	Which (ones) of your books did he want?
3. **Birisi gitti mi?**	Did somebody go?
4. **Birçoğunu anlamadım.**	I didn't understand a good deal of it.
5. **Geçen sene buraya gelmediler, değil mi?**	Last year they didn't come here, did they?
6. **Gelecek sene ne olacak?**	What will happen next year?
7. **Evimize gelmediği için parayı ona vermedik.**	Because he didn't come to our house, we didn't give him the money.
8. **Ahmedin dün gelmediğini söylediniz.**	You said that Ahmet didn't (hadn't) come yesterday.
9. **Ahmedin dün geleceğini söylediniz.**	You said that Ahmet would (was going to) come yesterday.
10. **Ahmedin bugün geleceğini dün söylediniz.**	Yesterday you said that Ahmet would (will) come today.
11. **Ahmedin yarın geleceğini size söyliyecekler.**	They'll tell you that Ahmet is coming (will come) tomorrow.
12. **Gördüğümüz adamın evi yok mudur?**	Doesn't the man whom we saw have a house?
13. **Söylediklerinden yarısını anlamadım.**	I didn't understand half of the things that they said.

14. Babası Ankaraya gidecek olan çocuk hasta oldu.	The child whose father is going (will go) to Ankara took (became) sick.
15. Ankaraya gidecek olanlar istasyona saat 7den evvel gelsinler.	People who are going to Ankara should come to the station before 7:00.

---

1. The partitive

The English partitive construction, e.g., 'one of a number,' 'part of a whole' has as its usual Turkish counterpart this pattern.

onlardan biri   one of them (from them)

The ablative expresses the idea 'from the whole'; the incomplete possessive construction (no expressed first member) expresses the part.

aralarından biri   one of them (from their midst)

In this usage, a word may bear what appear to be two possessive suffixes.

aralarından birisi   one of them

The word *birisi* also means 'someone,' 'somebody.'

Birisi gitmiş.	(Apparently) somebody went.
Birisi gitti.	Somebody (definitely) went.

Similar forms include

bazı	some	*bazısı*	some of it, of them
kim?	who?	*Kimi geldi, kimi gelmedi.*	Some of them came and some didn't.
başka	other	*bir başkası*	another of them, some other one
hep	all	*hepsi*	all of it, of them
		hepiniz	all of you
her	each, every	*her biri*	each one (of them)
birçok	a lot	*birçoğu*	a lot of it (of them)
	Compare	*birçokları*	a lot of them

2. Participles

The third person singular, positive and negative of the (a) general verb forms, (b) past indefinite verb forms, and (c) future verb forms may be used as verbal adjectives (participles).

akar su	water which flows; running water
okumuş (olan) bir adam	man who has read; educated man

(*olan*—present participle of *olmak*—may be used or omitted as one chooses.)

gelecek sene (or) *gelecek olan sene*	next year, coming year, year that will come
geçmiş zaman	time that has passed; past tense
bitmez iş	work that does not end; endless task
seni anlıyacak bir kız	a girl who'll understand you

Any participle, when it modifies no expressed word, may become a substantive and, in that event, may take suffixes.

yazarın evi	the writer's house
yazarların evleri	the writers' houses
Olacak oldu.	What was to happen happened.

The present participle is formed by the suffix -(y) V^2 n added to the positive or negative verb stem.

NOTE: The buffer (y) alters an immediately preceding a to $ı$, and an immediately preceding e to i.

POSITIVE		NEGATIVE
giden	going, one who goes	*gitmiyen*
bilen	knowing, one who knows	*bilmiyen*
anlıyan	understanding, one who understands	*anlamıyan*
istiyen	desiring, one who desires	*istemiyen*

A participle (verbal adjective) not only modifies words (its adjectival function) but also may exert verb force (can require other words to take suffixes).

oraya giden adamlar	(the) men who go there
Ankaraya gidenler	those who go to Ankara
Ankaradan gelen iki kadın	(the) two women coming from Ankara

3. Gerund in -t/d V^4 k

The gerund (verbal noun) in -t/d V^4 k is almost always second member of a possessive construction. The principal exception to this is when such a gerund is governed by the postposition *sonra* 'after.'

gittikten sonra	after going, after having gone.

The time value of this gerund varies. It may express present or past time. The third person singular future serves as the future gerund.

geldiğimde	when I come, came, do come, did come, etc.

106

her gittiğimde	at my every going, whenever I go, went, etc.
gelmediğinizden dolayı	because of your not coming, not having come, etc.
Ahmedin gelmiyeceğinden dolayı	because Ahmet isn't going to come, won't come

4. Indirect discourse

The gerund in -t/d V^4 k (for past and present tenses) and the future gerund (for the future tense) are the usual ways of expressing indirect discourse. The usual verb indicating indirect discourse is *söylemek* (*söyler*). That of direct discourse is *demek*. Study carefully the following examples.

1. Ahmet, 'Mehmet paramı aldı,' dedi.	Ahmet said, 'Mehmet took my money.'
2. Ahmet, Mehmedin parasını aldığını söyledi.	Ahmet said that Mehmet had taken his money.
3. Ahmet, 'Mehmet hırsızdır,' dedi.	Ahmet said, 'Mehmet's a thief.'
4. Ahmet, Mehmedin hırsız olduğunu söyledi.	Ahmet said that Mehmet's a thief.
5. Ahmet, 'Mehmet paranızı alacak, Selma,' dedi.	Ahmet said, 'Selma, Mehmet'll take your money.'
6. Ahmet, Selmaya Mehmedin parasını alacağını söyledi.	Ahmet told Selma that Mehmet will (would) take her money.

NOTE: In the above examples of indirect discourse, the subject of the dependent indirect construction becomes first member of a type I possessive construction, e.g., in sentences 2, 4, and in 6 the noun *Mehmedin*.

Note the type II possessive construction when the gerund is governed by a postposition.

| *Babam, Ahmet gelmediği için bana yazdı.* | My father wrote me because Ahmet didn't come. |

5. Relative gerundive and adverb

When the verb form in -t/d V^4 k modifies an expressed word, this form serves as verbal adjective (gerundive). This form seldom appears without some other suffix or suffixes added.

Used with possessive suffixes, this gerundive is called the relative gerundive.

Turkish has no single words equivalent to the English relative pronouns ('who,' 'which,' 'that') or the English relative adverbs ('when,' 'where').

The boy who came. The girl whose mother came. The house that I saw. The day when we went. The house where I found you.

For the Turkish interrogative pronouns and adverbs, to be distinguished from the relatives, see Lesson 7, section 2, Lesson 8, section 5.

The English nominative (absolute, subject of a verb) relative pronoun is expressed in Turkish in the participle. As an attributive adjective the participle precedes the noun.

gelen adam	man who is coming, who comes
gelecek adam	man who will come
akar su	water that (which) flows

An English possessive or objective relative pronoun is expressed in Turkish in the relative gerundive with a possessive suffix.

OBJECTIVE RELATIVE PRONOUN

	gördüğüm adam	(the) man whom I saw
full form:	*benim onu gördüğüm adam*	
	gördüğün adam	(the) man whom you saw
full form:	*senin onu gördüğün adam*	
	gördüğü adam	etc.
	gördüğümüz adam	
	gördüğünüz adam	
	gördükleri adam	

POSSESSIVE RELATIVE PRONOUN

	kitabını aldığım adam	(the) man whose book
full form:	*benim onun kitabını aldığım adam*	I took
	kitabını aldığın adam	(the) man whose book
full form:	*senin onun kitabını aldığın adam*	you took
	kitabını aldığı adam	etc.
	kitabını aldığımız adam	
	kitabını aldığınız adam	
	kitabını aldıkları adam	

NOTE: In indirect discourse the interrogative pronoun (*kim?* 'who?') appears as follows:

1. *Ahmet, 'Kim geldi?' dedi.*   Ahmet said, 'Who came?'

108

2. *Ahmet kimin geldiğini sordu.*   Ahmet asked who had come
                                     (who came).

3. *Ahmet bu kitabın kimin olduğunu*   Ahmet asked whose book this
   sordu.   was.

RELATIVE ADVERBS

geldiğim gün	(the) day (when, on which) I came
geldiğin zaman	(the) time (when, at which) you came
gitmediği halde	in (the) event that he didn't go, although he didn't go, hasn't gone, hadn't gone
geldiğim gibi	as soon as I came

Second only to the possessive construction (see Lesson 10), the greatest
difficulty with which Turkish confronts the English speaker is the expression
of the possessive and objective relative pronouns and of the relative adjectives.
Careful study of the patterns given above will do much to smooth the student's
path.

Exercises

A. Practice aloud. Translate.

1. Yeni gelenin ismi ne(dir)?
2. Ahmedin dün geldiğini bana söylemediler.
3. Sizin paranızı bulacağınızı ümit ettik.
4. Evinizi kiraya verdiğiniz adamın ismi ne?
5. Bunlardan hangisini istediler?
6. Bunu iyi bilenler az(dır).
7. Beyoğluna gitmek istiyenler kaç kişi?
8. Kimin geldiğini görmediniz mi?
9. Öğretmen, çocuklarımızın derslerine çok çalıştıklarını bize söyledi.
10. Babam, Ahmet buraya gelmediğinden dolayı bana bir mektup yazdı.
11. Gördüğünüz şehirlerden hangisi en güzel?
12. Dün gelmiş olan adamın otomobilini evimin önünde görmediniz mi?
13. Evini satın aldığınız kadın Fransaya gitti mi?
14. Buraya bir kaç defa geldikleri halde onlara hiç bir şey vermedik.
15. En güzel elmaları kimin satın aldığını söyledi mi?
16. Böyle bir şey yüz senede bir olmaz.

17. Kapıda kimi gördün?
    Birisi bundan yarım saat evvel gelmiş, efendim.
18. Trene binecek olanlar burada beklesinler.
19. Trene binecek olanların burada bekliyeceklerini söyledi.
20. Ahmedin parasını bulan kızın annesi parayı bana verdi.

B. Write in Turkish. Practice aloud.

1. Who (is it who) wants the biggest of these apples?
2. What is the name of the woman to whom you sold your house?
3. Where did the man whose house you bought live?
4. Who broke the cup into which I had put the milk?
5. Ahmet didn't see who came.
6. Ahmet said he didn't see who came.
7. Ahmet asked me who was coming.
8. After phoning you I left the house.
9. Because you know Turkish well, will you please write them a letter?
10. He said that he would write them a letter.

110

Lesson 17

-ki. Ki. Çünkü. The Professional Doer.

The Habitual Doer. Diminutives. Noun of Manner

---

1. **Dünkü yağmur çok iyi oldu.**

2. **Bunlar seninkiler mi?**
3. **Babanız gazeteci midir?**
   Hayır. Kitapçıdır.
4. **Yazıcınız buraya gelsin, bu yazdığı mektubu bana okusun!**

5. **Ahmedin söylediğine göre, gelmiyecekler.**
6. **Bir parçacık ekmek yemez misiniz?**
7. **Kadıncağız gelmesin!**

8. **Ufacık topla oynadılar.**
9. **Giriş (kapısı) hangi tarafta?**
10. **Öğretmen çocuğunuzun çok anlayışlı olduğunu söyledi.**

Yesterday's rain was certainly good.

Are these yours?
Is your father a journalist?
No, he's a book dealer.
Have your secretary come here and read me this letter that she (he) wrote!

According to what Ahmet says (said), they won't come.
Won't you eat just a tiny bit of bread?
I (we) hope that the poor woman won't come!

They played with a tiny ball.
Where (which way) is the entrance?
The teacher said that your child is very perceptive.

---

1. *-ki*

The suffix *-ki* (an element which does not conform to vowel harmony) has three principal uses.

111

a. Attached to a substantive, it forms an adjective.

sabahki hava	morning weather
evvelki gün	previous day
dünkü yağmur	yesterday's rain

With *dün* 'yesterday' and *gün* 'day' *ki*- does conform to vowel harmony.

b. Attached to a locative suffix, it forms an adjectival expression.

Amerikadaki çocuklar	(the) children in America, (the) children who are in America
ağaçtaki çiçekler	(the) flowers in the tree, (the) flowers which are in the tree
Ağaçtakiler güzeldir.	The ones in the tree are pretty.
Bu fotoğraflardakilerden misiniz?	Are you one of those who are in these photos?

c. Attached to the possessive forms of nouns and personal pronouns, *-ki* produces the equivalents of English 'X's,' 'mine,' 'yours,' etc.

Ahmedinki nerede?	Where is Ahmet's?
O benimkidir.	That's mine.
Benimkiler bunlar.	These are mine.
Seninki nerededir?	Where's yours?
Onunki yoktur.	He hasn't got one.
Bu onunkidir.	This one is his.
Bizimkiler bunlar.	These are ours.
Bu bizimkidir.	This is ours.
Onlar sizinkiler, değil mi?	Those are yours, aren't they?
Onlarınkiler nerede?	Where are theirs?
Onlarınki bu mudur?	Is this one theirs?

When further suffixes are attached to forms in *-ki*, a buffer *n* is used.

Ahmedinkini kim gördü?	Who has seen Ahmet's?

2. *Ki*

The Persian relative 'kih' 'that' has been taken into Turkish as *ki*, along with its grammar.

İsmi Hasan olan bir adam vardı.	There was a man whose name was Hasan.
Contrast *Bir adam vardı ki ismi Hasan idi.*	There was a man whose name was Hasan (that his name was . . .).

112

Ki sometimes 'ends' an unfinished expression.

O kadar gördük ki!   We saw so much that (I can't begin
to tell you)!

3. Çünkü

The Persian 'çünkü' 'because' also imports non-Turkish grammar into Turkish.

Hava fena olduğu için gitmedik.	Because the weather was bad, we didn't go.
Contrast *Gitmedik çünkü hava fena idi.*	We didn't go, because the weather was bad.

NOTE: *Zira*, also borrowed from Persian, is used in the same way as *çünkü*. Foreigners learning or using Turkish should avoid overuse of *ki, çünkü,* and *zira*. No matter how aptly the non-Turk may use these words, he will always be vulnerable to the charge 'That's not Turkish.'

4. The professional doer

The suffix -ç/c V⁴ added to a noun forms the noun which names the individual 'who does,' the professional. This suffix is frequently followed by -l V⁴ k to form the name of the profession.

gazete newspaper	*gazeteci* journalist	*gazetecilik* journalism
banka bank	*bankacı* banker	*bankacılık* banking, the banking business
kitap book	*kitapçı* bookseller	*kitapçılık* the book business

5. The habitual doer

The suffix -(y) V⁴ c V⁴ added to a verb stem forms the noun of the habitual doer, the individual who customarily or habitually performs the action involved, or who incites others to do so.

| *yazıcı* | writer, secretary, scribe (from *yazmak* 'to write') |
| *görücü* | (looker) the matchmaker of old-fashioned Turkish life, go-between (from *görmek* 'to see') |

6. Diminutives

Turkish makes extensive use of diminutives. They indicate smallness, affection, sarcasm, or contempt. The usual suffix is -ç/c V^4 k.

oda	room	*odacık*	little room
Hasan		*Hasancık*	little Hasan, good old Hasan, pal Hasan
Mehmet		*Mehmetçik*	Turkey's GI Joe, Tommy Atkins
şair	poet	*şaircik*	poetaster, poetizer

A final *k* may drop out before the diminutive suffix.

ufak	small	*ufacık*	tiny
küçük	little	*küçücük*	tiny
mini	tiny	*minicik*	very tiny
		mini minicik	minuscule

Another diminutive suffix is -ç/c V^2 ğ i/ı z. It is usually used pityingly.

kadın	woman	*kadıncağız*	poor woman

7. Noun of manner

The suffix -(y) V^4 ş added to a verb stem forms the noun of manner.

gidiş	going, way of going
anlayış	penetration, way of understanding
giriş	entrance, way of going in
çıkış	exit, way of leaving

Exercises

A. Practice aloud. Translate.

1. Sizin gelmemenize rağmen, Ahmet parayı istemiyecek, değil mi?
2. Saati demir kutunun içinde bulacaksınız.
3. Anahtarı kapıcıdan alacağım, değil mi?
4. Otomobilin yok mu?
5. Fahrünnisanın o gün geleceğini bilmediler, değil mi?
6. Hangisini istedi?
7. Bunlar onunkiler değildir.
8. Renginin bembeyaz olduğunu söyledi.

9. Bunlardan en güzelini istediği bellidir.
10. Selma, buraya geldiği gün, Fahrünnisaya iki kilo kahve verdi.
11. Benimkiler sizinkilerden iyidir.
12. Okuduğunuz kitabı nereye koyduğunuzu söylemez misiniz?
13. Okuduğum, kitap değildi. Ben bir haftalık mecmua okudum.
14. O adamın parası çokmuş. Babası da zenginmiş.
15. Babası zengin olduğu halde, Ahmedin çok parası yokmuş.
16. Buraya geldikten sonra, lisanı çok çabuk öğreneceksiniz.
17. Otomobilimi ona sattığım adamın kızının ismi Selmadır.
18. Ben onu görür görmez, Ahmet geldi.
19. Evinizdeki kitaplardan hangilerini alsınlar?
20. Bu küçücük halıya kaç para istedi?
21. Giriş nerede?
22. Erdoğanın söylediğine göre, onların evi çok güzelmiş.
23. Bu, böyle olacak bir şey değildir.
24. 'Ahmedin bana verdiği kitabı okumam' demeyin.
25. Mehmet, Ahmedin ona verdiği kitabı okumamıştı.
26. Bu evin kirası kaç?
    Bu ev kiralık değildir.
    Efendim, bütün şehirde kiralık ev yok mu?
    Çok az var, fakat caminin karşısında iki tanesini bulacaksınız.
    Size göre, ikisinden hangisi daha iyi?
    Fikrimce, küçüğü iyidir.
27. İçtikleri suyu beğenmediler.
28. Sinema nasıl idi? Onu beğendiniz mi?
29. Yanlarındakiler kimler?
30. Onlar İstanbullu değillermiş, Antalyadan gelmişler.
31. Böyle şeyler söyliyecek bir kadın değildir.
32. Eski evlerin iki kısmı vardır: birisi selâmlık, yani erkeklerin kısmı; diğer kısım harem, yani kadınların kısmı.
33. Çocukluğumdan beri sinemaya hiç gitmedim.
34. 'Gelsin! Gelsin!' desinler. Ben gitmem.
35. Ondan hiç haber olmadığını söyliyecekler.

B. Write in Turkish. Practice aloud.

1. Mother dear, please come here!
2. The apple trees in my garden are larger than those in yours.
3. The photographers all went to Ankara together.
4. This building has three exits.

5. Selma told me that her father is going to buy a new car.
6. Since Mehmet didn't come, I hope that Ahmet won't come either.
7. Doesn't your father have a secretary?
8. I didn't like the movie we saw last night.
9. Because the weather is very bad, we're not going to go to see them.
10. How much money did he want for the one in the bedroom?

Lesson 18

Progressive Verb Forms.

Common Infinitive plus the Locative with 'to Be.'

Ordinals and Distributives. Gerundive in -(y) V^2

---

1. **Ne diyorsunuz? Ahmet gitsin mi, gitmesin mi?**	What do you say? Ought Ahmet to go or not?
2. **Nereye gidiyorlar?**	Where are they going?
3. **Beş seneden beri Türkiyede oturuyorduk.**	We had been living in Turkey for five years.
4. **Ankarada mı oturuyor?**	Does he live in Ankara?
5. **Gazeteyi okumakta idiler.**	They were reading the paper.
6. **Ahmet İstanbula geldiği gün, ben Ankaraya dönmek üzereydim.**	The day Ahmet came to Istanbul, I was just ready to go back to Ankara.
7. **Atınız dokuzuncu geldi, sonuncu geldi.**	Your horse came in ninth—last.
8. **Çocuklarımız üçer sene Ankarada kaldılar.**	Our children spent three years each in Ankara.
9. **Ayın kaçında gelecek?**	What day of the month will he come?
10. **Ne diye bize gelmiyorsunuz?**	Why is it that you (never) come to see us?

---

1. Progressive verb forms

The progressive verb forms denote action still going on and not yet completed.

The suffixes of the present progressive verb forms are

	SINGULAR	PLURAL
1st	-(V)^4 y o r u m	-(V^4) y o r u z
2nd	-(V^4) y o r s u n	-(V^4) y o r s u n u z
3rd	-(V^4) y o r	-(V^4) y o r l a r

The symbol (V^4) in these forms denotes a vowel buffer. It is used after any positive verb stem which ends in a consonant. After a verb stem which ends in a vowel—this, of course, includes all negative verb stems—the (V^4) buffer is omitted.

The final vowel of any verb stem (positive or negative) which ends in e or a is altered by the immediately following initial y of the progressive suffixes. The verb stem's final e becomes i; its final a becomes ı. Hence the verb demek (der) forms diyorum 'I am saying,' etc.

The syllable yor is invariable and hence violates vowel harmony.

The past progressive verb forms use these suffixes

	SINGULAR	PLURAL
1st	-(V^4) y o r d u m	-(V^4) y o r d u k
2nd	-(V^4) y o r d u n	-(V^4) y o r d u n u z
3rd	-(V^4) y o r d u	-(V^4) y o r l a r d ı

Strictly, the present progressive verb forms gidiyorum means

> I am (now in the action of) going.
>
> (or) I (have been in the action of going and still) am going.

In ordinary use, however, gidiyorum frequently also may have a general sense.

> Her gün gidiyorum.   I am going daily.

The past progressive conveys the idea of 'used to be X-ing.'

> Gidiyorum.   I used to go (used to be in the action of going).

NOTE:

İki seneden beri bu mektepte çalışıyorum.	I have been working at this school for two years (and still am).
İki seneden beri o mektepte çalışıyordum.	I had been working at that school for two years (but no longer am).

PRESENT PROGRESSIVE VERB FORMS

		POSITIVE	INTERROGATIVE
singular			
	1st	gidiyorum	gidiyor muyum?
	2nd	gidiyorsun	gidiyor musun?
	3rd	gidiyor	gidiyor mu?

118

plural

1st	gidiyoruz	gidiyor muyuz?
2nd	gidiyorsunuz	gidiyor musunuz?
3rd	gidiyorlar	gidiyorlar mı?

	NEGATIVE	NEGATIVE INTERROGATIVE
singular		
1st	gitmiyorum	gitmiyor muyum?
2nd	gitmiyorsun	gitmiyor musun?
3rd	gitmiyor	gitmiyor mu?
plural		
1st	gitmiyoruz	gitmiyor muyuz?
2nd	gitmiyorsunuz	gitmiyor musunuz?
3rd	gitmiyorlar	gitmiyorlar mı?

2. Common infinitive plus the locative with 'to be'

Another present tense, much used in newspapers and narration, is the
common infinitive plus the locative plus the present tense of 'to be.'

	SINGULAR		PLURAL
1st	Gitmekteyim.	I am (in the act of) going.	Gitmekteyiz.
2nd	Gitmektesin.		Gitmektesiniz.
3rd	Gitmektedir.		Gitmektedirler.

The past tense of this form is

	SINGULAR	PLURAL
1st	Gitmekteydim.	Gitmekteydik.
2nd	Gitmekteydin.	Gitmekteydiniz.
3rd	Gitmekteydi.	Gitmekteydiler.

Note also this pattern.

gitmek üzere olmak	to be on the point of going
Gitmek üzereyim.	I'm just going, just about to go.
Gitmek üzereydim.	I was just about to go.

3. Ordinals and distributives

The ordinals ('1st,' '2nd,' '3rd,' etc.) are formed with the suffix -(V⁴) n c V⁴.
The distributives ('one by one,' 'by twos,' 'in threes,' etc.) are formed with
the suffix -(ş) V² r.

CARDINAL	ORDINAL	DISTRIBUTIVE
bir	birinci (ıinci)	birer
iki	ikinci (2nci)	ikişer
üç	üçüncü (3üncü)	üçer
dört (dördü)	dördüncü	dörder
beş	beşinci	beşer
altı	altıncı	altışar
yedi	yedinci	yedişer
sekiz	sekizinci	sekizer
dokuz	dokuzuncu	dokuzar
on	onuncu	onar
on bir	on birinci	on birer
yirmi	yirminci	yirmişer
otuz	otuzuncu	otuzar
kırk	kırkıncı	kırkar
elli	ellinci	ellişer
altmış	altmışıncı	altmışar
yetmiş	yetmişinci	yetmişer
seksen	sekseninci	seksener
doksan	doksanıncı	doksanar
yüz	yüzüncü	yüzer
bin	bininci	biner
on bin	on bininci	on biner

The distributives are frequently said twice.

Birer birer geldiler.   They came one by one.

Note also:

ilk	(the) first
son	(the) last
kaçıncı?	(the) how-manyeth?

4. Gerundive in -(y) V²

The suffix -(y) V² added to a verb stem makes a form comparable to the English verbal adjective in -*ing*.

koşmak	to run	*koşa*	running (adjective)
gülmek	to laugh	*güle*	laughing
Koşa koşa geldi.			He came on the run (running, running).
Güle güle gitti.			He went laughingly.

One says to a person who has a new garment

Güle güle giyiniz!　　　Wear it in happiness!

To a person who has a new abode

Güle güle oturunuz!　　　Live (dwell) there in happiness!

In Turkish, saying good-bye follows this pattern.

a. Allaha ısmarladık (usually contracted to Alasmaladık). 'Well, I have decided to depart, good-bye.' (lit. 'We have commended [you] to God.' This is said by the person who is leaving.)

b. Güle güle (gidiniz)! 'Good-bye.' (lit. '[Go] laughing, laughing,' response of the person of whom leave is being taken.)

NOTE: From demek 'to say' (used with direct quotations) comes the gerundive diye 'saying.'

| Kız 'Baban nerede' diye bana sordu. | The girl asked me, 'Where is your father?' |

Diye may represent a pair of 'spoken' quotation marks.

| Arkadaşlar diye söze başladı. | He began (his) speech with (the word) 'friends.' |
| Gitmek istemiyorum diye bağırdı. | He shouted, 'I don't want to go!' |

Diye may also mean 'on the pretext that,' 'on the supposition that.'

| Balık tutarım diye göle gitti. | He went to the lake, hoping (on the supposition) that he would catch some fish. |

Ne diye is a frequent expression for 'why?'

| Ne diye gelmediniz? | Why didn't you come? |

Exercises

A. Practice aloud. Translate.

1. Biz sinemaya gidiyoruz, Hasan Bey. Siz de gelmiyor musunuz?
2. Hangi sinemaya gidiyorsunuz?
3. Kristal Sinemasına gidiyoruz. Çok iyi bir filim oynuyor. Geliniz. Çok beğeneceksiniz.
4. Doğrusu, Mehmet Bey, ben sinemayı pek sevmiyorum. Aynı zamanda çok işim var.

5. Yazık, Hasan Bey, o halde siz işinizi görünüz. Biz gideceğiz. Allaha ısmarladık.
6. Güle güle, efendim. İnşallah filim çok iyidir. Belki önümüzdeki hafta ben de o filmi göreceğim.
7. Hasan Bey sinemaya gitmek üzereydi, fakat işi çok olduğundan vazgeçti, gitmedi.
8. Babası Pariste olan kızın ismini biliyor musunuz?
9. Biliyorum. İsmi Selmadır.
10. Babası Pariste kaldığı zaman, Selma nerede oturacak?
11. Şimdiki halde yanımızda oturuyor. Gelecek ay, babası Fransadan döndükten sonra, onunla beraber kendi evlerinde oturacak.
12. Çocuklar mektepten ikişer ikişer çıktılar.
13. Biz hep yirmişer lira verdik.
14. Mihri, Mehmedin yarın geleceğini söylüyor.
15. Siz hakikaten geleceğine inanıyor musunuz?

B. Write in Turkish. Practice aloud.
1. This evening my father is working at home. Therefore I hope that he will give me the key to the car.
2. What are you doing?
3. I am writing a letter to my sister.
4. Are you writing to your sister in Ankara or to the one in İzmir?
5. To the one in İzmir.
6. I was on the point of going to Bursa, but my father didn't give me the money.
7. Believing that Ahmet had taken his book, Mehmet phoned Ahmet's father.
8. Sait writes to the effect that Ahmet will come tomorrow.
9. I'm going home. Good-bye, Mehmet.
10. Good-bye, Ahmet.

Lesson 19

'To Be Able'

---

1. **Söylediklerimi anlıyabildiniz, değil mi?**	You were able to understand what (the things that) I said, weren't you?
2. **Benimle gelebilir misin?**	Can you come with me?
3. **Gelemem.**	I can't (come).
4. **Olacak mı?**	Will it happen (work, turn out well)?
5. **Olabilir. Olabilir.**	It may. It may (happen, etc.).
6. **Olamaz!**	Impossible! (It cannot happen, etc.)
7. **Ben gidemez miyim?**	Can't I go? (Do you mean to say that I can't go?)
8. **Okuyabildiğim kitaplar çoktur, okuyamadığım kitaplar azdır.**	The books I've been able to read are numerous; those that I haven't been able to read are few.
9. **Ahmet gelemiyeceğini söyliyecek, fakat gelebilecek.**	Ahmet will say that he won't be able to come, but he'll be able to.
10. **İstediklerinizi bulamadılar.**	They couldn't find (the things) what you wanted.

'To be able'

The gerundive in -(y) V²—and not the verb stem—is the base on which various compound verb forms are built. Of these the most important are the forms composed of the gerundive in -(y) V² plus *bilmek*, the device by which

123

Turkish expresses the idea of 'to be able' ('to know how to'). In the negative, tense and person suffixes are added directly to the negative gerund. Forms of *bilmek* are not required.

common infinitive

	POSITIVE		NEGATIVE
gidebilmek	to be able to go, being able to go	*gidememek*	not to be able to go, not being able to go

past definite

singular

1st	gidebildim	gidemedim
2nd	gidebildin	gidemedin
3rd	gidebildi	gidemedi

plural

1st	gidebildik	gidemedik
2nd	gidebildiniz	gidemediniz
3rd	gidebildiler	gidemediler

past definite interrogative

singular

1st	gidebildim mi?	gidemedim mi?
	etc.	etc.

general forms

singular

1st	gidebilirim	gidemem
2nd	gidebilirsin	gidemezsin
	etc.	etc.

general interrogative

singular

1st	gidebilir miyim?	gidemez miyim?
2nd	gidebilir misin?	gidemez misin?
	etc.	etc.

future

singular

1st	gidebileceğim	gidemiyeceğim
2nd	gidebileceksin	gidemiyeceksin
	etc.	etc.

future interrogative

    singular

1st	**gidebilecek miyim?**	**gidemiyecek miyim?**
2nd	**gidebilecek misin?**	**gidemiyecek misin?**
	etc.	etc.

past indefinite

    singular

1st	**gidebilmişim**	**gidememişim**
2nd	**gidebilmişsin**	**gidememişsin**
	etc.	etc.

past indefinite interrogative

    singular

1st	**gidebilmiş miyim?**	**gidememiş miyim?**
2nd	**gidebilmiş misin?**	**gidememiş misin?**
	etc.	etc.

present progressive

    singular

1st	**gidebiliyorum**	**gidemiyorum**
2nd	**gidebiliyorsun**	**gidemiyorsun**
	etc.	etc.

present progressive interrogative

    singular

1st	**gidebiliyor muyum?**	**gidemiyor muyum?**
2nd	**gidebiliyor musun?**	**gidemiyor musun?**
	etc.	etc.

past progressive

    singular

1st	**gidebiliyordum**	**gidemiyordum**
2nd	**gidebiliyordun**	**gidemiyordun**
	etc.	etc.

past progressive interrogative

    singular

1st	**gidebiliyor muydum?**	**gidemiyor muydum?**
2nd	**gidebiliyor muydun?**	**gidemiyor muydun?**
	etc.	etc.

3rd person imperatives

	singular	gidebilsin!	gidemesin!
	plural	gidebilsinler!	gidemesinler!

gerund in -t/d V⁴ k

gidebildik   *gidemedik*

NOTE: The final *e* of a verb stem, positive or negative (e.g., *iste* and *isteme*) becomes *i* before the immediately suffixed *y*. The final *a* of a verb stem, positive or negative (e.g., *anla, anlama*) becomes *ı*.

istiyebilmek   *istiyememek*
anlıyabilmek   *anlıyamamak*

The negative general and future participles of the 'to be able' verb forms express the English 'too *x* to.'

kutuya giremiyecek kadar büyük   too big to go into the box

Exercises

A. Practice aloud. Translate.

1. Otomobil daha çabuk gitmez mi?
   Daha çabuk gidemez.
2. Pasaportunuzu aldıktan sonra oraya gidebilirsiniz.
3. Caddedeki otomobilin kimin olduğunu bilmiyor musunuz?
4. Yarın gelebileceğinizi ümit ediyoruz.
5. (tramvayda)
   Ön tarafa geçiniz, baylar. Orada boş yer çoktur. Burada inmek istiyen var mı? Galatasarayda inecek var mı?
6. (telefonda)
   Alo, Alo! Orası neresi, efendim?
   Burası İhsan Şirketi, efendim.
   Ahmet Bey orada mı?
   Hangi Ahmet Beyi istiyorsunuz, efendim?
   Bay Ahmet Mehmetoğlu.
   Hayır, efendim. Burada yokmuş. Her halde çıkmış. Bundan yarım saat evvel buradaydı.
   Siz kimsiniz, efendim?
   Ben Erdoğan Yılmaz.
   Erdoğan Bey! Siz misiniz?
   Benim, efendim. Ya siz?
   Ben Ankaralı Sait. Bugün geldim.
   Maşallah, Sait Bey. Hoş geldiniz!

126

Hoş bulduk, Erdoğancığım. Nasılsın? İyi misin? İnşallah iyisin.
Teşekkür ederim, Sait, çok iyiyim. Ya sen, sen nasılsın?
Ben de iyiyim teşekkür ederim. Ne var ne yok, Erdoğancığım?

* * *

Eyvallah, Erdoğan Bey. Bir randevum var. Allaha ısmarladık. Ahmet Beye
yarın tekrar telefon edeceğimi lûtfen söyler misin?
Hay hay! Sait Bey. Söylerim. Güle güle, efendim!

7. Yaşlı kadın ağlıya ağlıya oturdu.
8. Çocuklarımın arkadaşlarından en küçüğü budur.
9. Onlara göre siz oraya iki defa gitmişsiniz.
10. Türkiyede göreceğiniz şehirlerden en büyüğü İstanbuldur.
11. Ahmet, iki güzel halı satın aldığını yazdı.
12. Evinizin arkasında iki büyük ağaç mevcut olduğu doğru mudur?
13. Ahmet! Al bu parayı! Koşa koşa tütüncüye git, çabuk iki gazete al!
14. Gazeteleri alanın ismini biliyor musunuz?
15. Bu dünyada bundan daha güzel bir dağın mevcut olduğuna inanmıyorum.
16. Bu adam ne iş görüyor? Gazeteci midir? Öğretmen midir?
17. Süheylânın kızkardeşinin bizde iki üç gece kalacağını ümit ediyoruz.
18. Ne diye gelmedin, Ahmet?
19. Her sabah saat 9:30da buraya gelebileceksiniz, değil mi?
20. Her sabah buraya gelebileceğinize inanmam.

B. Write in Turkish. Practice aloud.

1. Ahmet said, 'I can't find my book.'
2. Ahmet said that he couldn't find his own book.
3. I hope that you can write me every week.
4. Why weren't you able to enter the building?
5. Will you be able to go to Ankara tomorrow?
6. May I come in?
7. I know you will be able to read this well.
8. Do you know why they weren't able to come?
9. It is evident that Ahmet won't be able to find the car key.
10. I can say that this is the best book I have ever read.

Lesson 20

Auxiliary Verb. Optative-Subjunctive.

Necessity. Condition

1. **Süheylâ kimden bahsediyordu?**
   Whom was Süheylâ talking about?
2. **Ne yapıyorsunuz? Yazı yazıyorsunuz, değil mi?**
   What are you doing? You're writing, aren't you?
3. **Geçen sene çok kar yağdı.**
   It snowed a lot last year.
4. **Ne dersiniz? Yağmur yağacak mı, yağmıyacak mı?**
   What do you say? Is it going to rain, or not?
5. **Gideyim mi?**
   Should I go? (Ought I to go? *Shall* I go?)
6. **Gidelim mi, gitmiyelim mi?**
   Shall we go, or not? (Should we go, or not?)
7. **Gitmeli değil miydik?**
   Didn't we have to go?
8. **Gitmemeliyim.**
   I must not go.
9. **Gitmek mecburiyetindeydim.**
   I had to (was obliged to) go.
10. **İstanbulda ise hava çok güzeldi.**
    In Istanbul, however, the weather was very fine.
11. **Oğlum, çalışmaktansa futbol oynamayı tercih etti.**
    My son preferred to play football, instead of working.
12. **Kimse bilmez.**
    Nobody knows.

13. **Ne kadar para istersen iste! Ben sana beş kuruş vermem.**
Ask for as much money as you want! I won't give you five *kuruş*.

---

1. Auxiliary verb

Etmek (*eder*) is the usual auxiliary. An older auxiliary is *eylemek*. Both mean 'to do' and both are seldom used except as auxiliaries. The usual word for 'to do' is *yapmak* ('make,' 'do,' 'manufacture').

The auxiliary is used with numerous nouns, especially with Arabic infinitives.

teşekkür etmek	to thank (to do the action *teşekkür* 'to render thanks')
bahsetmek	to discuss, talk about (with ablative), to mention

The old verb *kılmak* ('make,' 'do') today seldom appears except in the expression

namaz kılmak   to perform the formal Moslem prayer ritual.

Yapmak sometimes is used as an auxiliary, especially when the auxiliary is in the relative gerundive form.

Ahmedin yaramazlık yaptığı gün

Some originally Arabic words, with the aid of no auxiliaries at all, retain their grammatical force, i.e., require suffixes on preceding words.

denize nazır bir oda   a room looking onto (with dative) the sea

Turkish frequently uses the cognate object.

yazı yazmak	to write (writing)
yemek yemek	to eat (food)

Sometimes a cognate subject is used.

Yağmur yağıyor.   It's raining. (Rain is raining.)

2. Optative-subjunctive

The ideas of 'may' and 'might' can be expressed by the optative-subjunctive verb forms. Their suffixes, added to the gerundive (and not to the verb stem), are

	SINGULAR	PLURAL
1st person	-y i/ı m	-l i/ı m
2nd person	-s i/ı n	-s i/ı n i/ı z
3rd person	$-V^2$	-l V^2 r

PRESENT OPTATIVE-SUBJUNCTIVE VERB FORMS

		POSITIVE		NEGATIVE
singular				
	1st person	gideyim	that I may, might go	gitmeyeyim
	2nd person	gidesin		gitmeyesin
	3rd person	gide		gitmeye
plural				
	1st person	gidelim		gitmeyelim
	2nd person	gidesiniz		gitmeyesiniz
	3rd person	gideler		gitmeyeler

INTERROGATIVE

		POSITIVE	NEGATIVE
singular			
	1st person	gideyim mi?	gitmeyeyim mi?
plural			
	1st person	gidelim mi?	gitmeyelim mi?

Rather than the third person present optative-subjunctive forms, Turkish favors the use of the third person imperatives. (See Lesson 7, section 4.)

PAST

The optative-subjunctive past forms are seldom used. For the expression of hopeless wishes use of the conditional is more common.

		POSITIVE		NEGATIVE
singular				
	1st person	geleydim	I should have gone	gelmeyeydim
	2nd person	geleydin		gelmeyeydin
	3rd person	geleydi		gelmeyeydi
plural				
	1st person	geleydik		gelmeyeydik
	2nd person	geleydiniz		gelmeyeydiniz
	3rd person	geleydiler		gelmeyeydiler

INTERROGATIVE

		POSITIVE	NEGATIVE
singular			
	1st person	geleydim mi?	gelmeyeydim mi?
	2nd person	geleydin mi?	gelmeyeydin mi?
		etc.	etc.

3. Necessity

English 'have to,' 'must,' 'obliged to,' etc., are most frequently expressed by the suffix

$$-m \ V^2 \ l \ i/\iota$$

added directly to the verb stem (positive or negative) and followed by the required form of the verb 'to be.'

PRESENT

		POSITIVE		NEGATIVE
singular				
	1st person	**Gitmeliyim**	I have to go.	**Gitmemeliyim**
	2nd person	**Gitmelisin**		**Gitmemelisin**
	3rd person	**Gitmeli(dir)**		**Gitmemeli(dir)**
plural				
	1st person	**Gitmeliyiz**		**Gitmemeliyiz**
	2nd person	**Gitmelisiniz**		**Gitmemelisiniz**
	3rd person	**Getmeli(dir)ler**		**Gitmemeli(dir)ler**

PRESENT INTERROGATIVE

		POSITIVE	NEGATIVE
singular			
	1st person	**Gitmeli miyim?**	**Gitmemeli miyim?**
	2nd person	**Gitmeli misin?**	**Gitmemeli misin?**
	3rd person	**Gitmeli mi(dir)?**	**Gitmemeli mi(dir)?**
plural			
	1st person	**Gitmeli miyiz?**	**Gitmemeli miyiz?**
	2nd person	**Gitmeli misiniz?**	**Gitmemeli misiniz?**
	3rd person	**Gitmeliler mi?**	**Gitmemeliler mi?**

The third singular forms may be used impersonally.

Oraya gitmeli.	It's necessary to go there.
	One should (has to) go there.
Oraya gitmemeli.	It's necessary not to go there.
	One should not go there.

Compare with this usage the following patterns.

Oraya gitmek lâzım(dır).	It is necessary to go there.
Oraya gitmek gerek(tir).	It is right (proper, necessary) to go there.

The noun *mecburiyet* 'obligation,' 'necessity' furnishes another frequently used means of expressing necessity.

Gitmek mecburiyetindeyim.	I must go. (I am in the necessity of going.)
Gitmek mecburiyetinde miydiler?	Did they have to go? (Were they in the necessity of going?)

4. Condition

The sign of the conditional has two forms.

    a. -s V^2 (suffix)

    b. *ise* (independent word)

The conditional sign may follow a substantive.

o ise,	he, however; as for him; if he (i.e., if you mean him . . .)
kitapta ise	in the book, however; if in the book (i.e., if you mean in the book . . .)
ne ise, neyse	nevertheless; even so; be that as it may
her neden ise, her nedense	for whatever reason
(her) nasılsa	some way or other
yoksa	or else
kimse	nobody, no one (used with other negatives), someone
Evde kimse yok.	There's nobody home.
Kimseyi bulamadım.	I couldn't find anybody.

Note particularly this pattern

gitmektense	rather than going
Ben, sinemaya gitmektense evde kalmayı tercih ettim.	Instead of going to the movies, I preferred to stay home.

The suffixes of the present conditional verb forms, added directly to the verb stem, positive or negative, are

	SINGULAR	PLURAL
1st person	-s V^2 m	-s V^2 k
2nd person	-s V^2 n	-s V^2 n i/ı z
3rd person	-s V^2	-s V^2 l V^2 r

PRESENT CONDITIONAL

		POSITIVE	NEGATIVE
singular			
	1st person	gitsem	gitmesem
	2nd person	gitsen	gitmesen
	3rd person	gitse	gitmese
plural			
	1st person	gitsek	gitmesek
	2nd person	gitseniz	gitmeseniz
	3rd person	gitseler	gitmeseler

Used alone—in an unfinished condition or in a question—these forms may mean 'Wouldn't it be a good idea if . . . ?'

Haydi, ne dersin?	Well, what do you say? Wouldn't it be nice
Kalksak, denize girsek?	if we got up and went into the water?
O gitmese mi?	Is there any reason why he shouldn't go?

GENERAL CONDITIONAL

The general conditional verb forms are frequently used in expressing such indefinites as English 'whoever,' 'whatever,' 'wherever,' and 'whenever.'

Kim isterse gitsin.	Whoever wants to go, may.
O ne söylerse söylesin, doğru değildir.	No matter what he says (whatever he may say, let him say [it]), it's not so.
O kız nereye giderse gitsin, ben Ankaraya gitmem.	No matter where that girl goes, I'm not going to Ankara.
(Her) ne zaman giderse gitsin, ben geleceğim.	No matter when he goes, I'll come.

The interrogative may also express a condition.

Beni gördü mü kaçar.	When he sees me, he runs off.
	If he sees me, he flees.

Exercises

A. Practice aloud. Translate.

1. **Niçin yemeğinizi yemediniz?**
2. **Siz ne dersiniz efendim, oraya bugün gideyim mi, gitmeyeyim mi?**
3. **Kim gelirse gelsin, ben bu kitabı yalnız Ahmet Beye vereceğim.**
4. **Siz hakikaten bir saat sonra gitmeli misiniz?**

133

5. Elinizdeki saate şöyle bir bakarsanız, saatin 9:30 olduğunu göreceksiniz.
6. Yarın hiç kimsenin buraya gelemiyeceğinden korkarım.
7. Onlar derhal buraya gelmek mecburiyetinde değildiler.
8. Niçin telefon edemediğini biliyor musunuz?
9. Şehrimizde kar yağmaz.
10. Erdoğanın karısı, kendi annesinin iki ay kadar çok hasta olduğunu, fakat ondan sonra tekrar Ankaraya gittiğini söyledi.
11. Siz ne söylerseniz söyleyiniz, onların gitmeye hazır olduklarını kendi gözlerimle gördüm.
12. Büyük kutunuzdan aldığı saati size tekrar vermezse hakikati annesine söylemek mecburiyetinde kalacaksınız, değil mi?
13. Nasıl isterse öyle yapsın!
14. Haydi, çocuklar! Vakit geçiyor. Haydi gidelim.
15. Efendim, müsaadenizle ekmeğinizden ufak bir parça alayım mı?
16. Oğlum, okula gitmektense sinemaya gitmeyi tercih etti.
17. Ahmedin dün bize tarif ettiği kitapçı dükkânının nerede olduğunu bilmiyorsunuz, değil mi?
18. Gitmediğini söylemediler, değil mi?
19. Gitmiyeceğini söyleyemediler, değil mi?
20. Gelemiyeceğinden haberiniz yok mu?

B. Write in Turkish. Practice aloud.

1. May I give you a cup of tea, sir?
2. If I don't go, won't you go either?
3. What shall we talk about?
4. Did you really have to go?
5. Do you really have to go?
6. What do you say? Ought we to go, or not?
7. If he comes, we'll give him the book.
8. They, however, could not go.
9. Say, 'Thank you, sir!'
10. He didn't have to give us the money.

Lesson 21

Passive Verbs. The Agent.

Causative, Reflexive, and Mutual Verbs

---

1. **Bu kitap kimin tarafından yazıldı?**
   By whom was this book written?
2. **Gitmemize müsaade edilecek mi?**
   Will permission be given for us to go (for our going)?
3. **Anlatabildim mi?**
   Have I succeeded in making myself clear (in explaining myself)?
4. **Bunun sebebi bilinmez.**
   The reason for this is not known.
5. **Onlar hiç görüşmezler.**
   They never talk to each other.
6. **Bu yemeğe alıştım.**
   I grew accustomed to this food.
7. **Bize onu sormadılar.**
   They didn't ask us that.
8. **Çocuk yıkandı.**
   The child washed himself.
9. **Çocuğu yıkadık.**
   We bathed the child.
10. **Bana hiç bir şey öğretemedi.**
    He was unable to teach me a thing.

---

1. Passive verbs

The formation of the passive depends upon the final sound of the verb stem.

a. Most verbs whose stems end in a vowel form the passive by adding *n*.

söylemek	to say	*söylenmek*	to be said
okumak	to read	*okunmak*	to be read

b. Most verbs whose stems end in a consonant other than -*l* form the passive by adding -V^4 l.

kırmak	to break (transitive)	*kırılmak*	to be broken
vermek	to give	*verilmek*	to be given

c. Verbs whose stems end in -*l* form the passive by adding -V^4 n.

bilmek	to know	*bilinmek*	to be known
bulmak	to find	*bulunmak*	to be found

NOTE: *bulunmak*, 'to be found' (and 'to find one's self,' cf. French *se trouver*) is frequently used to mean 'to be' or 'to exist.'

The negative forms of the passive present no difficulties.

söylememek	*söylenmemek*
okumamak	*okunmamak*
kırmamak	*kırılmamak*
vermemek	*verilmemek*
bilmemek	*bilinmemek*
bulmamak	*bulunmamak*

The passive is very frequent in Turkish. It has two principal functions.

a. that of the English passive

Saatim nerede bulundu?	Where was my watch found?
Saatim kırıldı.	My watch was broken (was smashed).

b. that of the English active intransitive of such verbs as 'to break.' Note that English 'to break' has two meanings: a transitive meaning which requires an object—'I broke my watch.' and an intransitive meaning which requires no object—'My watch broke.'

Turkish *kırmak* 'to break' (transitive) expresses only the first of these meanings ('I broke my watch.') To express the second ('My watch broke.'), Turkish uses the passive. Hence the Turkish passive may have two connotations.

Saatim kırıldı.	My watch was broken.	(passive)
Saatim kırıldı.	My watch broke.	(active intransitive)

136

Many intransitive (active voice) Turkish verbs may take a passive form, thereby expressing the English impersonal.

olmak, olunmak
Rica olunur (or Rica edilir).   It is requested.
gitmek, gidilmek
İstanbula nasıl gidilir?   How does one go to Istanbul?

Confusion seldom arises between

    Saatim kırıldı.   My watch was smashed.
and   Saatim kırıldı.   My watch broke.

2. The agent

Ambiguity may always be avoided by expressing the agent with the passive. The agent is shown by the noun *taraf* in a possessive construction plus the ablative.

(benim) tarafımdan	by me	(sizin) tarafınızdan	by you
(senin) tarafından	by you	onların tarafından	by them
onun tarafından	by him (her, it)	otomobil tarafından	by the auto-
(bizim) tarafımızdan	by us		mobile

Another means of expressing the agent is the suffix -ç/c V².

   hükümetçe   by (the) government

3. Causative verbs

Most verbs form the causative by adding -t/d V⁴ r.

from bilmek, bildirmek   to inform, assert, announce, communicate; to cause (someone) to know (something), etc.
 Bunu ona bildirdiler.   They caused this to be known to him.
       They informed him of this.
 Bu ona bildirildi.   This was made known to him.

Verbs whose stems end in a vowel add only a -t.

 from anlamak, anlatmak   to explain, recount, etc.
  Mektubu bana anlattı.   He explained the letter to me.
  Mektup bana anlatıldı.   The letter was explained to me.

Verbs whose stems end in ç or ş add -V⁴ r.

from içmek, içirmek	to cause (someone) to drink (something)
Sütü çocuğa içirdiler.	They made the child drink the milk (got the child to drink it, gave it to the child to drink).
Çocuklara süt içirilir.	Children are made to drink milk (are given milk to drink).

Polysyllabic verb stems ending in *r* or *l* add only a -*t*.

from *oturmak, oturtmak*	to cause someone to sit down or dwell in (with objective definite)
Beni Ankarada oturttular.	They made me live in Ankara (settled me there, got me quarters there, stationed me there, etc.).
Ankarada oturtuldum.	I was made to live in Ankara.

The negative forms of the causative present no difficulties.

bildirmek	bildirmemek
bildirilmek	bildirilmemek
anlatmak	anlatmamak
anlatılmak	anlatılmamak
içirmek	içirmemek
içirilmek	içirilmemek
oturtmak	oturtmamak
oturtulmak	oturtulmamak

4. Reflexive verbs

Reflexive verb forms usually add the suffix -(V⁴) n.

giymek	to wear (clothes: transitive)
giyinmek	to dress oneself
giyindirmek	to clothe (someone else)
giyindirilmek	to be clothed (by someone else)

5. Mutual verbs

The mutual or reciprocal verb forms add the suffix -(V⁴) ş. The basic connotation is mutuality of action.

çarpmak	to hit, strike against (with dative)
çarpışmak	to collide, (for two or more) to hit each other
çarpıştırmak	to cause to collide with each other

çarpıştırılmak	to be caused to collide
görmek	to see
görüşmek	to converse, talk together
görüşülmek	to be conversed about
görüştürmek	to make to converse with each other
görüştürülmek	to be made to converse with each other
bulmak	to find
buluşmak	(for two or more) to meet together
buluşturulmak	to be caused to meet or get together

NOTE: A verb may be reciprocal in form although its meaning today retains little if any trace of the idea of mutuality.

kaçmak	to flee
kaçışmak	(for all) to flee, run off in different directions
gelmek	to come
gelişmek	to flourish, to develop (intransitive)
almak	to take
alışmak	to accustom, familiarize oneself with (with dative), become accustomed to (with dative)

Exercises

A. Practice aloud. Translate.

1. Çay fincanı kırılmış mıydı?
2. Bana göre o hakikaten bilinmez bir şeydir.
3. O adam tarafından yazılan kitaplar bu günlerde güçlük ile bulunuyor.
4. Dün Ahmet Beyoğlunda bulundu.
5. Fincan tarafınızdan mı kırıldı?
6. Haber hükümetçe resmen bildirilmiş.
7. Beni bir iskemleye oturttular ve gitmeme müsaade etmediler.
8. Ben gitmeliyim, efendim. Zaten geç kaldım. Şimdilik, Allaha ısmarladık. Güle güle, Mehmet Bey. Yine görüşürüz, inşallah.
9. Büyük kutu kapıdan geçmedi. Onun için pencereden indirildi.
10. O adamın evimize hiç gelmediği söylenemez. Üç beş defa geldi.
11. Ahmet hakkında iki saat konuştuk. Ondan sonra karar verdik. Her şey anlaşıldı.
12. Onlar ne söylerlerse söylesinler, biz oraya gitmene müsaade etmeyiz.

13. Size yardım edeyim, efendim!
14. İki tane üçüncü mevki bilet istiyorum, lûtfen.
15. Kendi söylediklerinizi unuttunuz mu?
16. Bu ev kimin tarafından yapıldı?
17. Parayı nereye koyduklarını sormadınız mı?
18. Bana onu sormayın!
19. Denizde yıkandılar.
20. İzmire Cuma günü gitmek mecburiyetinde kalırsam ne yapacağımı bilmiyorum.
21. Bu yeni fabrikalar geliştirilmektedir.
22. Söylenildiğine göre o İstanbuldan hiç dönmiyecek.
23. Çalışmazsanız öğrenemiyeceksiniz.
24. Size Türkçeyi kim öğretiyor?
25. Eski Türkçedeki 'talebe' kelimesinin yerine bugün 'öğrenci' kelimesi daha çok kullanılıyor.

B. Write in Turkish. Practice aloud.

1. This water is undrinkable (not to be drunk).
2. We'll meet in Adana next week. It's agreed (understood).
3. This tobacco is imported from Turkey.
4. Ahmet had Mehmet import the tobacco.
5. One can't get to Izmir by this road.
6. The road is being caused to be widened.
7. Get dressed quickly, son!
8. This news was communicated by the government.
9. Be careful! That is fragile (breakable)!
10. His handwriting is illegible.

Lesson 22

Abbreviating Verb Forms. Attendant Circumstances.
Verb Form in -(y) V^4 n c V^2. Verb Form in -t/d V^4 k ç V^2

1. **Dün evinize gelip annenizi gördüm.**
   Yesterday I came to your house and saw your mother.
2. **Dün evinize gidip annenizi görmedim.**
   Yesterday I didn't go and see your mother.
3. **Dün Ahmede gitmeyip size geldim.**
   Yesterday I didn't go Ahmet's, I came to your place.
4. **Atatürk Bulvarından geçerken sizi gördüm.**
   I saw you as I was crossing Atatürk Boulevard.
5. **O İstanbula gelerek bir ev aradı.**
   He came to Istanbul and hunted for a house.
6. **Babasını görünce çok sevindi.**
   He was very happy when he saw his father.
7. **O, gazete okudukça kızar.**
   Whenever he reads (a) paper, he gets angry.
8. **Çocuk çok büyüdü.**
   The child grew a great deal.
9. **Selma iyileşti.**
   Selma improved.
10. **Ahmet birdenbire ihtiyarladı.**
    Ahmet grew old all of a sudden.

1. Abbreviating verb forms

Turkish has two time-saving devices to avoid the necessity of repeating lengthy verb endings in such sentences as 'They had come to the house, seen all their friends, and then gone back home.' Note that all the verbs in this sentence are identical in person, number, and tense.

a. The first of these devices is simply to omit part of the ending of each verb until the final verb is reached. Then the last verb gets the full set of suffixes, and these are understood as serving for all the verbs.

Efendim, sizi tebrik eder, teşekkür eder, saygılarımı sunarım. 'Sir, I congratulate you, thank (you), and tender my regards.' In its full form, the sentence would be: *Efendim, sizi tebrik ederim, teşekkür ederim ve saygılarımı sunarım.* With the abbreviating forms, no coordinate conjunction is used.

This device is not used with the past definite forms.

b. The second abbreviating device is -(y) V^4 p. In such a sentence as 'They came and saw.' the first verb receives only the abbreviating suffix, the second verb receives all necessary suffixes. The first verb is understood to bear all the suffixes of the second.

If both verbs in the sentence have a negative meaning, the first verb does not necessarily require the negative syllable. The negative of the second verb may serve for both. If the first verb is negative and the second positive, the -(y) V^4 p is used with the negative verb stem.

This device should never be used more than once in any sentence. No coordinating conjunction may intervene between the form with the abbreviating suffix and the second verb.

gidip gelmek	to go and come
O gün Ahmet okula gidip sizi gördü.	That day, Ahmet went to school and saw you.
O gün Ahmet sizi gelip görmedi.	That day, Ahmet didn't come and see you.
O gün Ahmet okula gitmeyip sizi gördü.	That day Ahmet didn't go to school but did see you.

The abbreviating verb plus the relative gerundive furnish the Turkish expression for 'whether or not.'

Onun gelip gelmediğini bilmiyorum.	I don't know whether or not he came (has come).

2. Attendant circumstance

Turkish has two participles to convey the idea of attending circumstance. The action expressed by the participle was (is, will be) simultaneous with that expressed by the following main verb.

a. The first of these two Turkish circumstantial participles employs the present participle of 'to be.'

> *iken* (independent word)
> or *-ken* (enclitic which ignores vowel harmony)

Ben burada iken Mehmet Ankara gitti.	While I was here, Mehmet went to Ankara.
Siz burada iken Hasan bize gelmiyecek.	While you're here, Hasan won't come to our house.

İken and *-ken* combine with many verb forms, especially with the general participle.

gider iken or *giderken*	while going
okur iken or *okurken*	while reading
Cebimde para yokken siz hiç bir şey istemiyeceksiniz.	So long as I have no money in my pocket, you won't ask for a thing.
Ben yapma yapma derken o ağlamaya başladı.	While I was (still) saying, "Don't! Don't!' he started to bawl.

Derken, used alone, means 'While X was still saying . . .' 'Before you could say Jack Robinson.'

Derken, Mehmet geldi.	Whereupon, Mehmet came.

b. The second of the Turkish circumstantial participles is formed by the suffix -(y) V² r V² k.

This form denotes an action or circumstance which accompanies the action expressed by the following main verb. Frequently the two verb forms best translate as coordinates.

Evime gelerek para istedi.	He came to my house and asked for money.
Evime gelerek beni bulamayıp gittiler.	They came to my house, couldn't find me, and went away.

143

3. Verb form in -(y) V⁴ n c V²

This suffix expresses the ideas of 'upon (his coming),' 'the moment that (he came),' etc.

Necdet sizi görünce kim bilir ne diyecek?
Who knows what Necdet will say when he sees you?

Çocuklar derslerini bitirince bahçeye gittiler.
The children went to the garden when they had finished their lessons.

With the postposition *kadar*, this suffix has the sense of 'until,' 'up to the moment that,' etc.

Siz gelinceye kadar ben burada kalacağım.
I'll stay here until you come.

4. Verb form in -t/d V⁴ k ç V²

This form expresses the ideas of 'when,' 'whenever,' etc.

Onu gördükçe kız ağladı.
Whenever she saw it, the girl wept.

Onu gördükçe ağlar.
Whenever he sees it, he weeps.

5. Derived verbs

The four principal means by which verbs are derived from substantives or modifiers are

a. THE SUFFIX -l V²

ihtiyar	aged
ihtiyarlamak	to grow old
ihtiyarlatmak	to age (transitive)
ihtiyarlatılmak	to be caused to age
kolay	easy
kolaylamak	to facilitate; (of a task) to be almost done (intransitive); to get (a task) almost finished (transitive)
kolaylatmak	to make (a task) easy
kolaylanmak	(of a task) to become easier (or) nearly finished
kolaylandırmak	to make or permit (a task) to become easy of execution (or) nearly finished
kolaylaştırmak	to make (something) become easier; gradually to get (a task) nearly finished
kolaylaştırılmak	(for something) to be made easier and easier; (for a task) to be got to the place where it is almost done

144

b. The suffix -l V² n

beyaz	white
beyazlanmak	to grow white
beyazlatmak	to bleach, whiten (transitive)
beyazlatılmak	to be bleached, whitened
ümit	hope
ümitlenmek	to become hopeful
ümitlendirmek	to make (someone or something) hopeful
ümitlendirilmek	to be made hopeful

c. The suffix -V² l

az	few, little
azalmak	to diminish (intransitive)
azaltmak	to reduce or lessen
azaltılmak	to be diminished
çok	much, many, very
çoğalmak	to increase (intransitive), to grow
çoğaltmak	to increase (transitive), to make grow, to augment
çoğaltılmak	to be increased, be made grow
Compare *küçük*	small
küçülmek	to grow smaller
küçültmek	to make smaller, belittle
küçültülmek	to be made smaller, belittled

d. The suffix -l V² ş

bir	one
birleşmek	to come together, meet together, unite (intransitive)
birleştirmek	to bring together, unite (transitive)
birleştirilmek	to be brought together, united
iyi	good, well
iyileşmek	to get better, get well, improve (intransitive)
iyileştirmek	to make better, make well, improve (transitive)
iyileştirilmek	to be made better, well; to be improved

NOTE: Study of the above forms will demonstrate that they are parts of a living, human (and therefore illogical) speech, not of a rigid system. Therefore, the student's goal should be not to attempt to coin new forms 'by rule,' but to learn the forms which the Turks actually use.

Exercises

A. Practice aloud. Translate.

1. Ahmet Beyin yarın bizimle beraber sinemaya gidip gitmiyeceğini bilmiyorsunuz, değil mi?
2. Ben Beyoğlunda iken hırsızın biri evime girerek köpeğimi susturup iki güzel halı ile beş yüz lira aldı.
3. Çocukları susturamadıklarından dolayı öğretmenler onların babalarına birer şikâyet mektubu yazdılar.
4. Maşallah, Erdoğan Bey! Oğlunuz ne kadar büyüdü! Gözlerime inanamıyorum.
5. Arkadaşlarınızdan hangilerinin gelebileceklerini bilmediğimiz için yemeği hangi lokantada yiyeceğimize henüz karar vermedik.
6. Süheylâ Hanımın hastaladığından beri kaç ay geçtiğini iyice hatırlıyamıyorum.
7. Benim o gün gelemiyeceğimi onlar çoktan beri biliyorlardı. O halde onların bunu size niye hatırlatmadıklarını bir türlü anlıyamıyorum.
8. Kız babasını görünce hem koşmaya hem ağlamaya başladı.
9. Eğer İstanbulda iki haftadan fazla kalmak mecburiyetinde kalırsam sizinle Ankarada buluşamam.
10. Annenin senin o hafta Ankarada bulunduğunu bilip bilmediğinden emin olmadığım için, orada çektiğim fotoğrafı ne ona gösterdim, ne de babana.
11. Oraya gitmeyip burada kalmaya karar verirlerse, size gönderilmesine söz verdiğim kitapları benden istiyeceklerinden eminim.
12. Ankarada oturmaktansa İstanbulda oturman daha mı iyi?
13. Bilindiği gibi bayram günlerinde kütüphaneye girilmez.
14. Kapı açılınca çocuklar yerlerine koşup oturdular.
15. Onlar, birleştirilmezlerse istediklerini yapamıyacaklar.
16. Doktor her gün kliniğine gider, hastalarını kabul ederdi.
17. Gitmezsen ne olur?
18. Oraya hiç gitmememe rağmen bana haftada bir mektup yazıyor, daima beni beklediklerini söylüyorlar.
19. Hava fena olduğu için yüzmeye gitmedik.
20. Görmenin inanmak olduğunu unuttunuz mu?

B. Write in Turkish. Practice aloud.

1. Opening the door, he got into his car and left.
2. Don't forget that the world has grown smaller.
3. Do you know whether Ahmet had read this book?

4. Working hard, he learned Turkish well.
5. Prices went up increasingly.
6. As he was leaving, he gave me a lira.
7. It will be very good if we go there and give him a little money.
8. They wanted not to go there but to stay here.
9. They decided not to go there but to stay here.
10. He says they have decided not to go there but to stay here.

Lesson 23

Statement on Verb Forms.

True and Untrue Conditions

1. Statement on verb forms

The student who has mastered the material presented in the preceding lessons will now recognize, understand, and begin to be able to use the fundamental patterns of Turkish. The following tabulation of possible verb forms should help him identify the many combinations he will encounter as he uses the language.

These eight basic forms of the Turkish verb are familiar.

3RD PERSON SINGULAR

1.	past definite	*gitti*
2.	general	*gider*
3.	future	*gidecek*
4.	past indefinite	*gitmiş*
5.	progressive (present)	*gidiyor*
6.	optative-subjunctive	*gide*
7.	verb of necessity	*gitmeli*
8.	conditional	*gitse*

Disregarding infinitives, imperatives, and participles, the above eight forms represent the eight principal categories—or eight main lines of inflection—needed for comprehension of the entire Turkish verb system.

To use a figure of speech from the vocabulary of music, we may assert that in the symphony or harmony of Turkish speech, these eight categories are the verb system's eight principal themes. In music any given theme may be played, with strikingly different results, in more than one key. In the same way, we may say that the Turkish language has three keys and that most of the above eight themes may be put into each of the three keys, again with strikingly different results.

The three keys in Turkish are: the antedating key, the disclaiming key, and the provisional key.

a. ANTEDATING FORMS

The antedating key is formed by adding the past forms (independent or suffixed) of the verb 'to be' (see Lesson 14) to the third person singular theme form.

When any one of the eight themes is put into the antedating key, the time value of that theme's forms is thereby moved backward one notch (is 'antedated').

b. DISCLAIMING FORMS

This key is formed by adding the indefinite forms of the verb 'to be' (independent or suffixed) to the third person singular theme form.

When a theme is put into this key, the speaker (or writer) disclaims any personal knowledge of the accurateness of the assertion he is making.

When the past indefinite theme is put into the disclaiming key, the result is the strongest possible disclaimer of responsibility for the validity of the assertion.

There are no past definite disclaiming forms. One cannot logically disclaim and vouch for accuracy in one verb form.

NOTE: The analogy of musical themes and keys must not be pushed too far. The forms of a Turkish verb theme may stand in more than one key at the same time. Thus, each of the disclaimed theme verb forms may—when desired—also be antedated.

c. PROVISIONAL FORMS

The last of the three keys—the provisional—is formed with the conditional of the verb 'to be.' The conditional theme, naturally, does not occur in this key and neither does the optative-subjunctive theme. Verb forms put into the conditional key express the ideas of proviso or supposition.

> Provided I go . . .
> Suppose I go . . .
> If I go . . ., etc.

2. True conditions

Conditions present two main types, true and untrue. The subject (i.e., the speaker or writer), speaking objectively, voices a simple 'if' without indicating or hinting whether he regards the proviso which he enunciates as being true or false, likely or unlikely, possible or impossible, etc.

In a true condition the conditional forms of the verb 'to be' (i.e., the provisional key) are added to the base (third person singular) of the appropriate verb of the protasis (the 'if' part of the condition). The apodosis (the 'why then' part of the condition) has its verb form exactly as that verb would be were no proviso stipulated at all.

True conditions can be classified according to the time value of the protasis verb.

Protasis verb is past.

> *Parayı gördü isen (gördüysen) bana söyle.*
> *Parayı gördü ise (gördüyse) bana söyliyecek.*
> If he saw the money, he'll tell me.
> *Parayı görmüş ise (görmüşse) bana söyliyecek.*
> If he saw (has seen) the money, he'll tell me.

Protasis verb is present.

> *O geliyor ise (geliyorsa) siz gitmelisiniz.*
> If he is (now) coming, you must go.

Protasis verb is future.

> *O Ankarada kalacak ise (kalacaksa) annesi hasta değildir.*
> If he is going to stay in Ankara, his mother is not sick.

NOTE: Many protasis verbs have a vague time value, present or future. For example,

> *Parayı istersen, söyle.*
> If you want the money, say (so).
> *Parayı bulamazsan söyle.*
> If you can't find the money, say so.
> *Adamı görürsen bana söyle.*
> If you see the man, tell me (so).
> *Adamı görürsen bana söyliyeceksin, değil mi?*
> If you see the man, you'll tell me, won't you?

3. Untrue conditions

The subject (i.e., the speaker or writer), speaking subjectively, not only says 'if' but also states or hints whether he regards the proviso he is enunciating as being true or untrue, likely or unlikely, possible or impossible, etc.

In an untrue condition, the protasis verb is conditional theme present (or) antedated.

150

The apodosis verb is general theme antedated (or) future theme antedated.

PROTASIS VERB	APODOSIS VERB
Paranızı bulsa	*onu size verirdi.*
Paranızı bulsaydı (bulsa idi)	*onu size verecekti.*

Each of the sentences means

If he had found your money, he would have given it to you.

(and the speaker indicates his own belief, namely, that X did not find the money).

Key to Exercises

Lesson 2

Exercise B.

1. How many kilos of meat?
2. a half kilo of coffee
3. a little water
4. one and one half kilos of sugar
5. several times
6. several kilos of apples
7. two hundred fifty grams of butter
8. five cups of tea
9. very little lemon
   very few lemons
10. twelve oranges
11. three and one half hours
12. thirty streets
13. two and one half liras
14. How many apples?
15. How many *kuruş*? how much?
16. three and one half apples
17. sixty seconds
18. sixty minutes
19. twenty-four hours
20. one day
21. seven days
22. four weeks
23. twelve months
24. three hundred and sixty-five days
25. one hundred years
26. two trees
27. three sons
28. How many kilos of sugar?
29. one half kilo of sugar
30. one hundred times
31. How much money?
    How much does it cost?
32. a little bit of money; inexpensive
33. How many lemons?
34. lots of apples (many apples)
35. one head
36. two hands
37. two feet
38. two eyes
39. very little lemon; very few lemons
40. two glasses of water
41. little water (not much water)
42. a little milk
43. very little milk
44. ten thousand kilometers
45. eight newspapers
46. half a glass of water
47. seven and one half hours
48. two slices of bread
49. three spoons of sugar
50. three 'breads' (three loaves of bread)

Exercise C.

1. *yarım kilo çay*
2. *üç kilo şeker*
3. *iki yüz gram et*
4. *bir dilim ekmek*
5. *iki fincan kahve*
6. *sekiz tane elma*
7. *kaç tane ev?*
8. *iki tane minare*

9. *bir cami*
10. *üç yıl*
11. *dört gün*
12. *iki hafta*
13. *altı ay*
14. *çok süt*
15. *biraz su*
16. *iki ekmek (iki tane ekmek)*
17. *iki dilim ekmek*
18. *çok az şeker*
19. *çok ağaç*
20. *üç ırmak*
21. *yetmiş yedi göl*
22. *üç şehir*
23. *altmış dört çocuk*
24. *yüz çocuk*
25. *bir göz*
26. *iki göz*
27. *iki ayak*
28. *otuz iki diş*
29. *bir baş*

30. *beş yüz elli beş gün*
31. *on beş yıl*
32. *on iki kız*
33. *on dokuz kere (on dokuz defa)*
34. *on altı bahçe*
35. *otuz beş gece*
36. *otuz altı gün*
37. *elli yedi buçuk gram*
38. *yüz lira*
39. *iki buçuk lira (iki lira elli kuruş)*
40. *iki bin kilovat*
41. *çok cami*
42. *Kaç tane cami?*
43. *bir çok cadde*
44. *çok su*
45. *az su*
46. *Kaç bardak su?*
47. *biraz su*
48. *dört defa (dört kere)*
49. *çok meyva*
50. *çok elma*

Lesson 3

Exercise A.

1. a lovely (beautiful) mother
2. That mother is pretty.
3. (The) child is very tall.
4. a very tall child
5. a young girl (daughter)
6. One girl is young. (One daughter is young.)
7. The young girl (daughter) is small.
8. This young girl is very little.
9. These two women are good.
10. twelve good ladies
11. This (one) is very small.
12. two old women
13. (The) two women are aged.
14. The two old ladies are short.
15. Father is good (well).

16. a good father
17. (the) two good fathers
18. The two fathers are well.
19. How many fathers?
20. How many days?
21. How many apples?
22. a nice day
23. Today is fine. (This day is good.)
24. This is a nice day.
25. (the) big car
26. two large cars
27. (The) two autos are big.
28. This is a small car.
29. (The) one car's new; the other's old.
30. The big car's new.
31. The other car's awfully old.

32. This (one) is very old.
33. This candy's very good. (This sugar is good.)
34. a little sugar
35. That lake is very large.
36. (the) two pretty lakes
37. (The) two lakes are charming.
38. little money (not much money)
39. This (sum of) money is very small.
40. a little money

41. (the) three cups of coffee
42. (the) three coffees
43. (the) three coffees
44. a good many cups (several cups, a number of cups)
45. several cups of tea
46. How much money? (How much?)
47. 35 liras and 15 *kuruş*
48. (the) five old houses
49. (The) five houses are old.
50. This (one) is extremely old.

Exercise B.

1. *büyük bir ayak*
2. *bir büyük ayak*
3. *iki büyük ayak*
4. *Bu ayak büyük.*
5. *Bir ayak büyük, diğer ayak küçük.*
6. *Kaç kadın?*
7. *iki yaşlı kadın*
8. *Bu iki kadın yaşlı.*
9. *İki yaşlı kadın kısa (boylu).*
10. *kısa boylu yaşlı iki kadın*
11. *güzel bir cadde*
12. *iki güzel cadde.*
13. *Bu şehir yeni, diğer şehir eski.*

14. *üç yüksek minare (üç tane yüksek minare)*
15. *bu eski ev*
16. *Bu ev yüksek.*
17. *Eski ev büyük, yeni ev küçük.*
18. *Kaç ev? (Kaç tane ev?)*
19. *Kaç küçük ev? (Kaç tane küçük ev?)*
20. *Kaç ev küçük? (Kaç tane ev küçük?)*
21. *Bu ev çok küçük.*
22. *Çok küçük ev güzel.*
23. *dört genç adam*
24. *Dört adam genç.*
25. *Dört genç adam uzun.*

Lesson 4

Exercise A.

1. Today is pleasant.
2. These days are good.
3. These cups are very small.
4. How many little cups?
5. How many cups are small?
6. Some cups are very big.
7. Those cups are lovely.
8. five cups of good coffee
9. This young child is very big.
10. This youth is very tall.

11. These young children are very small.
12. These youths are very short.
13. This cup's big.
14. This big cup is pretty.
15. These cups are beautiful.
16. These big cups are pretty.
17. The big ones are lovely.
18. These big ones are very good.

154

19. This house is small.
20. This little house is pretty.
21. These little houses are pretty.
22. The little ones are very nice.

Exercise B.
1. *bir at*
2. *bir büyük at*
3. *büyük bir at*
4. *büyük atlar*
5. *büyük atlar*
6. *iki büyük at*
7. *bazı büyük atlar*
8. *Bazı atlar büyük.*
9. *Bu büyük at çok iyi.*
10. *Diğer büyük at çok fena.*
11. *İki büyük at güzel.*
12. *Bu atlar küçük.*
13. *Büyükler çok iyi, küçükler fena.*
14. *iki yaşlı kadın*

23. The little ones are old (but) the big ones are new.
24. How many houses are small?
25. How many small houses?

15. *iki yaşlı kadın*
16. *bazı yaşlı kadınlar*
17. *bazı yaşlılar*
    bazı eski şeyler
18. *Bu kadın yaşlı, diğer kadın genç.*
19. *Eski şeyler küçük.*
    Yaşlılar küçük.
20. *Gençler güzel.*
21. *Fahrünnisa genç, Ahmet çok yaşlı.*
22. *Bu iyi.*
23. *Bu iyi.*
24. *Küçük evler eski büyük evler yeni.*
25. *Küçükler eski büyükler yeni.*

Lesson 5

Exercise A.

Note: Each past definite form may, according to the context, normally convey any one of the three English past tenses set forth above (Lesson 5, Section 3). Hence the 'translations' given below by no means convey the whole potential significance of the Turkish verb forms.

1. Who came?
2. When did you come?
3. They've read a lot.
4. You haven't read much. (said to one person)
5. I understood very little.
6. We didn't get (understand) much.
7. The youngsters ran a good deal.
8. The two children came this morning.
9. This coffee's very good.
10. I bought a kilo and a half of coffee.
11. Who laughed?

12. Erdoğan laughed a good deal.
13. How many times have you come? (How many times have you been here?)
14. Istanbul is a large and beautiful city.
15. The Mediterranean is large, (and) the Marmara is small.
16. The house is pretty and the yard (garden) is big.
17. The young people got here today.
18. (The) five youths laughed.
19. This child is very young.
20. The little girl ran.
21. two large eyes

155

22. The two eyes are large.
23. This eye is big, (and) that eye is small.
24. What's this?
25. This is an apple.
26. How many liters of milk?
27. two and one half cups of milk
28. Who are they?
29. They are Sait and Ali.
30. Who has understood? (Who's got the point?)
31. They understood.
32. These houses are large.
33. These are large.
34. The grownups got here this morning.
35. The youths have come this evening.

36. The fruit has ripened.
37. Ahmet wanted to come.
38. Ahmet, when did you come?
39. I came this morning.
40. The kids read a little.
41. What did they want?
42. How many cars did you see?
43. I saw five automobiles.
44. What has happened?
45. good children
46. When did you come?
47. The young folks ran.
48. What have you found?
49. two good children
50. What did they read?

Exercise B.

1. *büyük bir çocuk*
2. *Çocuk büyük.*
3. *dört küçük kız*
4. *Dört kız küçük.*
5. *beş güzel küçük kız*
6. *Bu beş küçük kız güzel.*
7. *üç büyük fena çocuk*
8. *Bu sabah fena bir çocuk geldi.*
9. *Fena çocuk bu sabah geldi.*
10. *Kim geldi?*
11. *Ahmet ne zaman geldi?*
12. *iki kilo portakal*
13. *iki kilo iyi portakal*

14. *Bu iki kilo portakal çok iyi.*
15. *Elmalar çok iyi, portakallar fena.*
16. *Süheylâ çok okudu.*
17. *Çok az aldık.*
18. *Bu şehir çok büyük.*
19. *Deniz ve dağlar güzel.*
20. *Cadde büyük, cami küçük.*
21. *Ne zaman geldiler?*
22. *Ahmet kaç tane elma istedi?*
23. *Yedi elma istedi.*
24. *Kaç kaşık şeker?*
25. *Kaç dilim ekmek?*

Lesson 6

Exercise A.

1. Who's taken the money? (Who took the money?)
   Ahmet took the money.
   Ahmet took it.
2. Who took the money?
   Ahmet did.
   When did he take it?

He took the money this morning.
He took it this morning.
He took (it) this morning.
3. Mehmet, when did you see Ahmet?
   I saw Ahmet today.
   I saw (him) today.

4. Children! Whom did you see today?
   Today we saw several men.
5. Who has seen these two men?
   We have seen them.
6. What did this little girl break?
   She broke a cup.
7. Who broke the cups?
   The little girl broke the cups.
   The little girl broke them.
8. When did the girl break the cups?
   She broke them this morning.
9. How many cups did the little girl break?
   She broke two cups.
   She broke two.
10. What did the dog see?
    The dog saw the cat.
    The cat ran.
11. What did the cat want?
    The cat wanted milk.
    What did the cat find?
    The cat found the milk.
12. Who took these five glasses?
    I took them.
    When did you take the glasses?
    I took the glasses this evening.

13. These mountains are very lovely.
    They saw the lovely mountains.
    They saw some lovely mountains.
14. Ahmet, when did you come?
    I came this morning.
    When did Ahmet come?
    He came this morning.
15. Mehmet and Sait came yesterday.
    Who came yesterday?
    Yesterday they came.
16. Who understood him?
    I understood him.
17. You are late, Ahmet!
    Yes, I am very late.
18. Istanbul is a large city.
    Who has seen Istanbul?
    We have seen it.
19. Those youngsters are very small.
    When did they go?
    The little ones went this morning.
20. Welcome, Ahmet! Come right in!
    Thanks, Mehmet! I'm glad to be here.

Exercise B.

1. *Dün kitabı okudum.*
2. *Dün iki kitap okudum.*
3. *Bu kitabı kim okudu?*
4. *Dün gittiniz. (Siz dün gittiniz.)*
5. *Hoş geldiniz, Fahrünnisa!*

6. *Hoş bulduk, Selma.*
7. *Mehmet biraz para istedi.*
8. *Mehmet kaç para istedi?*
9. *Parayı kim istedi?*
10. *İki lirayı buldum.*

Lesson 7

Exercise A.

1. Ahmet's got the car. (Ahmet took the car.)
2. It's Ahmet who's got the car. (Ahmet took the car.)
3. Who saw me? (Who's seen me?)
4. They wanted you. (They asked for you.)

5. I read that book (way over there) but you read this one.
6. We've seen the big mosque.
7. Whom did they ask for? (Whom did they want?)
8. Look, Mehmet, look! Ahmet's come.

9. Please take this fruit.
10. Drink the coffee!
11. Come here, Mehmet! Ahmet has smashed something!
12. Understanding this is very hard.
13. How many times did you see us?
14. When did they get here?
15. Find them.

Exercise B.

1. *Onu bul! Bul!*
2. *Gül!*
3. *Beni gördü ve ben onu gördüm.*
4. *Gelsinler!*
5. *Bunlar büyük.*
6. *İzmiri ve Eskişehir'i gördüm.*
7. *Büyükler bunlar.*
8. *Çocuk dün geldi.*

16. You knew it yesterday.
17. Who asked for such a thing? (Who wanted something like this?)
18. I went, I saw (it), I came (back).
19. Please read this book today.
20. If only they'd come quickly! (I wish they would hurry!)

9. *Bu hafta gittiler.*
10. *Bu ay çok güzel.*
11. *On beş lira otuz beş kuruş istedi.*
12. *On beş lirayı dün aldım.*
13. *İki büyük halı aldılar.*
14. *Bu çok güç.*
15. *Bunlar çok kolay. Bu şeyler çok kolay.*

Lesson 8

Exercise A.

1. How many people came from Ankara yesterday morning?
   Five people came.
   Where did they come from?
   From Ankara.
   Ahmet and Mehmet came too.
   Yes, they came too.
2. These rugs are very lovely, Ali.
   Yes, (they are) very lovely.
   Where did you find them?
   I found them in Istanbul.
   Where?
   In the Kapalıçarşı.
   How much did you get them for?
   I gave 500 liras for the big rug.
3. On Tuesday Ahmet Bey came to Istanbul. He went to the Covered Bazaar. There he saw many things. He bought two pretty rugs. Later, he went to Taksim. That night he stayed in a hotel at Taksim. Wednesday morning at eight he went back to Ankara from Istanbul.
4. The girl went to Izmir yesterday.
5. Where did she come from?

6. She came from Ankara.
7. Where did you see Ahmet?
8. Where is the dog?
9. I saw the dog in the garden.
10. One day a cat saw a dog. The dog saw the cat. The cat stared and stared at the dog. Suddenly the cat ran out of the garden. He ran away quickly. The dog returned home from the garden.
11. From whom did they take (receive) the money?
12. They took the money from Mehmet.
13. How much money did they take?
14. To whom did Ahmet give the fifteen liras?
15. He gave the money to them.
16. Who drank the milk?
17. What did you drink?
18. Mother and Father talked about Ahmet.
19. You came very late.
20. Yes, we have come very late.

158

Exercise B.

1. *Ben de o kitabı istedim.*
2. *Ahmet Pazar günü döndü.*
3. *İzmirde kimi gördüler?*
4. *Kaç kilo peynir istedi?*
5. *İki yüz elli gram peynir istedi.*
6. *Bu peynir çok iyi.*
7. *Dün nereye gittiler?*
8. *Bu sabah nereden geldiniz?*

9. *Çocuklara kim baktı?*
10. *Dün Selma onlara baktı.*
11. *Ağaçta neyi gördün, Erdoğan?*
12. *Ağaçta kediyi gördüm, baba.*
13. *Kutuda ne buldun, Erdoğan?*
14. *Kutuda on lira buldum.*
15. *Şekeri fincandan kim aldı?*

Lesson 9

Exercise A.

1. Ahmet! Didn't you go to school today?
2. No, Father. I didn't go to school today.
3. Did you go to the city?
4. No, Father. Today I didn't go either to school or to the city.
5. In that case, where did you go? What did you do?
6. I saw a garden. I went into the garden.
7. Which garden did you go into?
8. I didn't go to the big garden. I went into the small garden.
9. Have you been to Izmir? How long did you stay there?
   I stayed there two, two and a half months.
10. Ahmet, be a good boy! Go to school. Go every day. Work very hard.
    Have you understood (me), or not?
    I have understood, Father.
11. Have you ever been to Ankara?
    No, I've never gone there. I've certainly wanted to, but I've not gone. I haven't even been to Bursa. I've just seen one city—Istanbul. Have you been to Ankara?
    Yes, I've gone there lots. I've been to Izmir. I've gone also to Adana.
12. How many times have you been to Adana?
    To Adana? I've gone there five (or) six times.
    In short, you've traveled a lot.
    Yes, I have traveled a lot.
13. What did you think of Ankara? Is it pretty?
    Yes, Ankara is pretty.
    And Istanbul?
    Istanbul? It's pretty, too, very lovely.
14. Where did you come from today?
    Today I came from Adana.
    What day did you go (had you gone) there?
    I went there Saturday.
    What did you think of Adana?
    (It's) very big and very lovely. But it's hot!

159

15. Did they ask you for money, or not?
They did. They wanted 275 liras.
Did you give them the 275 liras, or not?
I wanted not to, but I did. Yesterday Ahmet gave (had given) me 300 liras.
Today I gave them the 275 liras.

Exercise B.

1. *Ahmet gitti mi?*
2. *Ahmet mi gitti?*
3. *Kitabı size verdiler mi? Hayır, vermediler.*
4. *Selma iki çocuğu gördü mü? Evet, gördü.*
5. *Niçin parayı bize vermediniz? İstemediniz mi?*
6. *Dün parayı Erdoğana verdim. Onu görmediniz mi?*
7. *Gelsinler mi, gelmesinler mi?*
8. *Ahmet niçin gelmesin?*
9. *Ne çay içti ne kahve.*
10. *Fahrünnisa hiç bir şey içmedi.*
11. *Hiç Ankaraya gittiler mi?*
12. *Hiç Ankaraya gittiniz mi?*
13. *İzmirden geldiler mi?*
14. *Hayır, oradan gelmediler. Adanadan geldiler.*
15. *Gazeteyi babaya verdiniz mi?*
16. *Evet, onu (ona) verdim.*
17. *Odada ne buldunuz?*
18. *Orada hiç bir şey bulmadım.*
19. *O kutuya ne peyniri koysun ne şekeri.*
20. *Ahmet gazeteyi okusun mu, okumasın mı?*

Lesson 10

Exercise A.

(Simple possessive constructions)

1. Ahmet's mother is very young.
2. Where's your house?
3. The child's father came.
4. Who's your father?
5. The city's water is quite good.
6. If only their father would come here!
7. It is to be hoped that their fathers won't go there!
8. Is this your book?
9. The rug owner took the money.

10. Whose apple is this?
11. The Turkish alphabet is easy.
12. Is Turkish difficult?
13. Is your garden pretty big?
14. Ankara Boulevard is lovely.
15. How lovely Ankara's boulevards are!
16. Is your bedroom small?
17. Our classroom is hot.
18. Does that woman own a car?
19. Where's the landlord?
20. Who owns this house?
21. My own book is in the house.
22. The landlord hasn't asked for the money.
23. They came Tuesday.
24. Where are the teacups? (or) Where are her/their teacups?
25. This textbook is very large.

Possessive complexes, etc.

1. Your father's eyes are handsome.
2. The trees of our city are very large.
3. Ahmet's two sons came.
4. Let the little child's mother come quickly!
5. The landlord's radio is a very good one.
6. Where's your landlord?
7. The house of your friend's mother is large.
8. We hope that our daughter's friends won't come here today.
9. Whose father's house is this?
10. What is your son's name?
11. Didn't they know their landlord's name?
12. Who should look after Ahmet's children?
13. I came through Beyoğlu's streets.
14. I put neither her books nor my own books into my sister's bedroom.
15. Didn't they take my books?
16. Don't give your father's money to the mother of those children!
17. Whom did you see at the Ankara kindergarten?
18. Haven't you seen my boy and Ahmet's two girls?
19. They took one book from my son.
20. It went from the Dardanelles to the Bosporus.
21. When did they go to Beyoğlu?
22. Have you ever seen the Taurus Mountains?
23. He didn't want his friend's book.
24. He wanted his own book.
25. Don't come to my house! Go to your friend's house!

Exercise B.

1. *Ders odamızda kimi buldunuz?*
2. *Ahmedin annesi çocukların yatak odasına girdi.*
3. *Kardeşimin ev sahibi otomobilini babamın garajına koydu.*
4. *Otomobil Beyoğlundan İstanbul Üniversitesine gitti.*
5. *Vapur Çanakkale Boğazından geçti.*
6. *Küçük kızkardeşinizin çay fincanları güzel.*
7. *Ev sahibimin kendi evi İstanbul Caddesinde.*
8. *Oğlunuzun ayakları büyük.*
9. *Küçük kardeşinizin ismi ne?*
10. *Ahmedin kızkardeşi dün gece niçin kızkardeşlerinizin evine gitmedi?*
11. *Hiç Beyoğluna gittiniz mi?*
12. *Ahmet Karadenizi hiç görmedi, fakat Marmara Denizini gördü.*
13. *Annemin parasını Mehmedin ve Erdoğanın kızkardeşlerine verdiler.*
14. *Küçük ders odasından çıktı, büyük ders odasına girdi.*
15. *İstanbul şehri çok eski. Ankara şehri yeni.*
16. *Yeni Türk alfabesi kolay.*
17. *Oraya hiç gitmeyin.*
18. *Boğaziçi çok güzel. Çanakkale Boğazı da güzel.*
19. *Hiç Çanakkale Boğazını gördünüz mü?*
20. *Dün Çanakkale Boğazına gitmediniz mi?*
21. *Otomobil Beyoğlu caddelerinden geçti. Karaköyden geçmedi.*
22. *Babasının evi Afyonkarahisar'da.*
23. *Bu adam otomobil sahibi mi?*
24. *Büyük otomobilin sahibi, o evin sahibinin kardeşine on lira verdi.*
25. *Arkadaşımın babasının otomobilinden kimen kitaylarını aldın?*

Lesson 11

Exercise A.

1. Sir, we are very eager for you to come to our home. We await you sir; we anticipate (it).
2. To go to New York takes a lot of money.
3. What a pity for Selma to break all of Fahrünnisa's coffee cups!
4. Father, I intend to go to the movies.
   Ahmet, have you studied your schoolbook? Is your lesson ready?
   I've studied hard, Father. I have read (it) twice.
   What do you say, Selma? Ought the boy to go to the movies tonight, or not?
   Certainly, Mehmet, let him go. Why shouldn't he go?
   All right, let him go. On your way now, Ahmet! But don't stay out late!
   Thanks, Father. And I thank you, too, Mother. I'll not be late.

5. What's the meaning of this, Ahmet? You've only got a six in your Turkish. What's happened? Didn't you work? Work hard! For that matter, it's always necessary to work in life. Have you understood or not? I have understood, Father. I'll work. I'll really work.

6. Will you have a (cup of) tea, sir? Thank you, no. I never drink tea. In that case, may it not be a (cup of) coffee, sir? I thank you, madam. Would you please give me a cup of coffee?

7. Ahmet Bey preferred to drink coffee rather than tea.

8. Ahmet read his textbook without getting the sense of a single word.

9. We hope you have (a) good trip, Ahmet Bey! Bon voyage! (May your road be open!)

10. Mehmet comes to our house each morning. It would be fine if his older brother Erdoğan would come, too.

11. We pay the ticketsellers on the buses; they hand us our tickets.

12. Each morning Ahmet Bey eats breakfast, reads the paper, and goes to his office.

13. Each morning Selma Hanım eats breakfast, cares for the house, and goes to market.

14. Ahmet Bey eats his lunch in a restaurant.

15. Do you drink tea?

16. No, sir. I never drink tea.

17. Selim Bey knows French well. He studied French at Istanbul University for three and one half years.

18. Has Ahmet come or not?

19. He hasn't come yet. But, he will come, sir. He will come.

20. This train leaves the station at eight o'clock.

Exercise B.

1. *Selma bir bardak süt içer mi?*

2. *Teşekkür ederiz, hanımefendi. Selma hiç süt içmez. Lûtfen, ona bir bardak su verir misiniz?*

3. *Selma, süt içmektense su içmeyi tercih eder.*

4. *Dün sabah Kapalıçarşıda Ahmet Bey iki güzel halı gördü.*

5. *İkisini de almak istedi.*

6. *Halı sahibi küçüğe iki bin lira, büyüğe beş bin lira istedi.*

7. *Ahmet Bey, 'O çok pahalı. İkisine dört bin beş yüz lira veririm,' dedi.*

8. *Adam, hiç beklemeden, 'Hayır. Ben ikisine yedi bin lira isterim,' dedi.*

9. *Neticede, Ahmet Bey Kapalıçarşıdan, halıları almadan çıktı.*

10. *O eve döner dönmez, eşi, 'Halı aldın mı?' dedi.*

11. *'Hayır, almadım. Halı sahibi iki güzel halıya yedi bin lira istedi. Çarşıdan halıları almadan çıktım,' dedi.*

12. *Eşi, 'Çok fena!' dedi.*

13. *Ahmet Bey, 'Ya yazık,' dedi, 'fakat o yedi bin lira istedi. Çok pahalı buldum.'*

14. *Eşi, 'Amma ben yeni halı isterim,' dedi.*

15. *Ahmet Bey, 'Evet şekerim,' dedi. 'Güzel bir halı bulmaya çalışırım.'*

Lesson 12

Exercise A.

1. My house is bigger than your house.
2. Will it be (a) good (thing) for Sait to come from America? Sait hasn't come from America yet. He will come in the month of June.
3. In that year we used to go to Ankara once a month.
4. Will you please give me the salt?
5. What do you say, sir; shall we go there or not?
6. Have they come to you (your house)?
   Yes, sir, they have come twice.
   Twice? In that case they'll come to our house, too.
   They certainly will.
7. Didn't you go to the Ahmet Beys'?
   I didn't. In fact, I never go there.
8. As soon as I opened the newspaper, this was what I saw.
9. The two youngsters started to run.
10. The girl's hair is jet black.
11. Reading lots of books is (a) good (thing).
12. The little girl's reading is good.
13. Who wrote these (writings)?
    I did.
    My boy, don't write like this! One must write better!
14. To whom do the best apples belong?
15. Are these yours?
16. My father gets up at 7:00, eats breakfast, reads the paper, gets into the car at 8:30, and goes to his office.
17. Doesn't he want to study?
    Not at all.
18. Aren't you going to go today?
19. No, but I'll go tomorrow.
20. To whom will you give these?
21. Ahmet won't go to Italy without having given me the money.
22. In your opinion, does (will, would) Ahmet take my money?
23. Shall Ahmet go to your mother's house tomorrow, or not?
24. They didn't come yesterday but they will come tomorrow.
25. Will you or will you not give us the money?

Exercise B.

1. *Niye Beyoğluna gitmiyeceksin?*
2. *Selmanın babası otomobilini kimden satın aldı?*
3. *Onu hangi garaja koyacak?*
4. *Hangi sinemaya gidecekler?*
5. *Mehmet hiç sinemaya gitmez.*

164

6. *Sinemaya haftada iki defa giderdik.*
7. *Bence, oğlunuzun bu kitabı okumaması fena(dır).*
8. *Onlar günlerce aradılar, fakat köpeği bulmadılar.*
9. *Kimi bekledin?*
10. *Seni yarın evimde bekliyeceğim.*
11. *Ankaraya gelir gelmez Mehmet Beye telefon ettim.*
12. *O, kitapları size vermeden Ankaraya gitmiyecek.*
13. *Köpeğim Selmanın köpeğinden (daha) büyük(tür).*
14. *Onun köpeği bembeyaz fakat benim köpeğim simsiyah.*
15. *Yavaş gidiniz!*
16. *İyi anlamadım.*
17. *En küçük kız en büyük elmayı yedi.*
18. *Ahmet gelecek mi, gelmiyecek mi?*
19. *Ahmedin fikrince Selma gelsin mi, gelmesin mi?*
20. *Niçin daha çok çalışmazsınız?*

Lesson 13

Exercise A.

1. Who passed behind us?
2. Won't they pass in front of us?
3. Who came after you (did)? Who came behind you?
4. Because of you, your brother also came late.
5. Why didn't you give me an apple like this one?
6. What did you find in the box?
7. He took the newspaper from his pocket.
8. His house is on the mountain's top.
9. The dog knows his master's voice.
10. They brought tea for me.
11. Why did they come before eight o'clock?
12. The child wrote with his father's pencil.
13. Why did you work?
14. We strove in order to understand, and to learn.
15. I have never read a book like this.

Exercise B.

1. *Ahmet cebine ne koydu?*
2. *Selma çay fincanlarını nerede buldu?*
3. *Kutuda bir fincan buldu, diğerlerini arkasında buldu.*
4. *Kitabımı kim aldı?*
5. *Ahmet aldı.*
6. *Nereye koydu?*

7. *Ağacın yanına koydu.*
8. *Nilüfer nerede?*
9. *Sinemaya gitti.*
10. *Yalnız mı gitti?*
11. *Hayır.*
12. *Kiminle gitti?*
13. *Ahmedin kızkardeşiyle gitti.*
14. *Geç kalacaklar mı?*
15. *Hayır, buraya saat dokuz buçuktan evvel gelecekler.*

Lesson 14

Exercise A.

1. Where's your car, Ahmet Bey?
2. I don't have a car, sir. I used to (I did have one), but I've sold it.
3. Was your car good, Ahmet Bey?
4. It wasn't good. It was very old. That's why I sold it.
5. Where's little Selma, Mihri Hanım?
6. She's not here. I haven't seen Selma today.
7. But she'll come here today, won't she?
8. Yes, Mihri Hanım, I hope she's going to come.
9. Who was at your house yesterday afternoon?
10. Mehmet was (there). Ahmet was (there). A few friends came in. We sat (around and) talked. That's all . . .
11. You have two sisters, don't you?
12. No, I have only one sister, but my husband has two sisters.
13. Are there apples in Turkey?
14. Yes, in fact there are lots of apples.
15. You have two apple trees in your yard, don't you?

Exercise B.

1. *Kimin kitabı bu? Bu kitap kimin(dir)?*
2. *Kimin kitabı yok(tur)?*
3. *Bunlar sizin, değil mi?*
4. *Bunlar sizin değil(dir), değil mi?*
5. *(Onun) dört kızkardeşi vardı, değil mi?*
6. *Senin kitabın evimde(dir).*
7. *Evlerinde kitap yok.*
8. *Ahmedin babasının iki otomobili var(dır).*
9. *Babanızın otomobili yoktu, değil mi?*
10. *Ahmet orada mı(dır)?*

Lesson 15

Exercise A.

1. Is your brother's bedroom upstairs or downstairs?
2. Have you seen our sister?
3. Who took the money from under the box?
4. Ahmet [the narrator says] came here yesterday morning, said this and said that, then took my sister's money and departed.
5. According to Ahmet, they don't come here.
6. We found two places in the front of the streetcar.
7. My boy, don't go indoors today!
8. Had he not gone to Istanbul before 1937?
9. The water came up to his mouth.
10. According to you, my sister did not get into Ahmet's car.
11. What else did they want? (Apart from that, what . . .)
12. Why won't they come?
13. They won't be particularly anxious to come here.
14. What did he put into the teacups?
15. The train stayed five minutes in the station.
16. You haven't gone to Turkey for a long time.
17. Does your house have a garden?
18. The youngsters started on a trip five days ago.
19. Is this house for sale or rent?
20. Istanbul has many daily newspapers.
21. Despite the fact that I am poor, I won't take money from that man!
22. Ahmet and Erdoğan (apparently) worked hard in order to go to Istanbul.
23. Do you want to keep the big box? (Should it stay with you . . .?)
    Yes, let it stay (here) for a week or so.
24. Don't cross in front of the train!
25. Children, please don't open the outside door!

Exercise B.

1. *Mehmet! Ahmet İstanbula gitti mi?*
   Onu görmedim. Fakat her halde gitmiştir.
   Erdoğan! Siz Ahmedi gördünüz mü?
   Gördüm, efendim. İstanbula gitmedi. Edirneye gitti.
2. *Kahveniz şekerli mi olsun, şekersiz mi (olsun)?*
3. *Ben limonlu çay severim.*
4. *Bu sütlü kahve çok iyidir.*
5. *Ahmedin kardeşi 1955 senesinden evvel ölmüş müydü?*
6. *1949 senesinde iki evim vardı. Şimdi üç tane var.*

7. *O zaman evli değildiniz, değil mi?*
8. *Babam daima iyilik, doğruluk ve güzellik istedi.*
9. *Ahmede göre gitmemiş.*
10. *Ahmede göre gitmemiş idi.*

Lesson 16

Exercise A.

1. What is the name of the newcomer?
2. They didn't tell me that Ahmet had come (came) yesterday.
3. We hoped that you would find your money.
4. What is the name of the man to whom you rented your house?
5. Which (one) of these did they want?
6. Those who know this well are few. (Not many people know this well.)
7. How many persons want to go to Beyoğlu?
8. Didn't you see who came?
9. The teacher told us that our children work (have worked) hard in their lessons (classes).
10. Because Ahmet didn't (hasn't) come here, my father wrote me a letter.
11. Of the cities you've seen, which one is the most lovely?
12. Didn't you see the car of the man who came yesterday, out in front of my house?
13. Has the woman whose house you bought gone to France?
14. Although they came here a number of times, we didn't give them anything.
15. Did he say who it was who bought the best apples?
16. This sort of a thing doesn't happen once in a hundred years.
17. Whom did you see at the door?
   Apparently somebody came a half an hour ago, sir.
18. Those who are going to board the train should wait here.
19. He said for the people who are going to get on the train to wait here.
20. The mother of the girl who found Ahmet's money gave the money to me.

Exercise B.

1. *Bu elmalardan en büyüğünü istiyen kimdir?*
2. *Evinizi sattığınız kadının ismi nedir?*
3. *Evini satın aldığınız adam nerede oturdu?*
4. *İçine sütü koyduğum fincanı kim kırdı?*
5. *Ahmet kimin geldiğini görmedi.*
6. *Ahmet kimin geldiğini görmediğini söyledi.*
7. *Ahmet kimin geleceğini bana sordu.*
8. *Size telefon ettikten sonra evden çıktım.*
9. *Türkçeyi iyi bildiğinizden dolayı onlara bir mektup yazar mısınız, lûtfen?*
10. *Onlara bir mektup yazacağını söyledi.*

Lesson 17

Exercise A.

1. Even though you didn't come, Ahmet won't ask for the money, will he?
2. You'll find the watch inside the iron box.
3. I'll get the key from the doorkeeper, won't I?
4. Don't you have a car?
5. They didn't know that Fahrünnisa was coming that day, did they?
6. Which one (of them) did he want?
7. These aren't his.
8. He said that its color was snow white.
9. It's clear that he wanted the prettiest one of these.
10. The day Selma came here she gave Fahrünnisa two kilos of coffee.
11. Mine are better than yours.
12. Won't you say where you put the book you read?
13. What I read (was reading) wasn't a book. I read a weekly magazine.
14. That fellow seems to have a lot of money. His father is wealthy, too.
15. Although his father is rich, Ahmet doesn't seem to have very much money.
16. After you have come here, you'll learn the language very quickly.
17. The name of the daughter of the man to whom I sold my car is Selma.
18. The minute I saw it (her, him), Ahmet arrived.
19. Which (ones) of the books in your house should they (ought they to) take?
20. How much money did he ask for this tiny rug?
21. Where's the entrance?
22. According to what Erdoğan says (said), their house is (should be) very nice.
23. This is not a matter which will happen in this fashion.
24. Don't you say, "I won't read the book Ahmet gave me!"
25. Mehmet had not read the book that Ahmet gave him.
26. How much does this house rent for?
    This house isn't for rent.
    Sir, in the entire city isn't there a house for rent?
    There are very few, but you'll find two of them over across from the mosque.
    In your view, which of them is the better?
    As I see it, the little one (of them) is the better.
27. They didn't like the water they drank.
28. How was the movie? Did you enjoy it?
29. Who are those people with them?
30. They seem not to be natives (or residents) of Istanbul; they're from Antalya.
31. She's not a woman who'll talk in such a fashion.
32. Old houses have two parts: one of them is the *selâmlık*, i.e., the men's section; the other part is the *harem*, i.e., the part for the women.

33. I've not been to the movies since I was a child.
34. (All right) let them say, 'If only he would come! If only he would come!' I'm *not* going to go.
35. They'll say that there's no news of him.

Exercise B.

1. *Anneciğim, buraya gelin, lûtfen!*
2. *Bahçemdeki elma ağaçları bahçenizdekilerden daha büyüktür.*
3. *Fotoğrafçılar hep beraber Ankaraya gittiler.*
4. *Bu binanın üç (tane) çıkışı vardır.*
5. *Selma, babasının yeni bir otomobil satın alacağını bana söyledi.*
6. *Mehmet gelmediği için Ahmedin de gelmiyeceğini ümit ederim.*
7. *Babanızın yazıcısı yok mudur?*
8. *Dün gece gördüğümüz filmi beğenmedim.*
9. *Hava çok fena olduğundan onları görmeye gitmiyeceğiz.*
10. *Yatak odasındakine kaç para istedi?*

Lesson 18

Exercise A.

1. We're going to the movies, Hasan Bey. Won't you come along, too?
2. What theater are you going to?
3. We're going to the Crystal. A very good film is playing. Come on! You'll have a great time.
4. To tell the truth (the truth of it is), Mehmet Bey, I don't particularly like movies. In addition, I've got a lot of work.
5. That's too bad, Hasan Bey. In that case, you take care of (do) your work. We'll be on our way. Good-bye.
6. Good-bye, sir. I hope the film is good. Perhaps next week I, too, will see that picture.
7. Hasan Bey was just about to go to the movies, but because he had a lot of work he changed his mind and didn't go.
8. Do you know the name of the girl whose father is in Paris?
9. I do. Her name is Selma.
10. While her father is staying in Paris, where will Selma live?
11. At present she is staying with us. Next month, when her father has come back from France, she'll live with him in their own house.
12. The children left the school two by two.
13. We all gave twenty liras apiece.
14. Mihri says that Mehmet is going to come tomorrow.
15. Do you really believe that he's coming?

170

Exercise B.

1. *Bu akşam babam evde çalışıyor. Onun için otomobilin anahtarını bana vereceğini ümit ediyorum.*
2. *Ne yapıyorsunuz?*
3. *Kızkardeşime bir mektup yazıyorum.*
4. *Ankaradaki kızkardeşinize mi İzmirdekine mi yazıyorsunuz?*
5. *İzmirdekine.*
6. *Ben Bursaya gitmek üzereydim, fakat babam parayı bana vermedi.*
7. *Mehmet, Ahmet kitabını aldı diye, Ahmedin babasına telefon etti.*
8. *Sait, Ahmet yarın gelecek diye yazıyor.*
9. *Ben eve gidiyorum. Allaha ısmarladık, Mehmet.*
10. *Güle güle, Ahmet.*

Lesson 19

Exercise A.

1. Won't the car go faster?
   It can't go any faster.
2. You can go there after you have received your passport.
3. Do you know who owns the car out there on the street?
4. We hope that you'll be able to go tomorrow.
5. (aboard a streetcar)
   Move up towards the front, gentlemen. There's lots of empty space there. Is there anyone who wants to get off here? Is there anyone who is going to get off at Galatasaray?
6. (on the telephone)
   Hello, hello! What number do I have, sir?
   This is the İhsan Company, sir.
   Is Ahmet Bey there?
   Which Ahmet Bey do you want, sir?
   Mr. Ahmet Mehmedoğlu.
   No, sir. He doesn't seem to be here. He must have gone out. He was here half an hour ago.
   Who are you, sir?
   I (am) Erdoğan Yılmaz.
   Erdoğan Bey! Is that you?
   It's me, sir. And you?
   I (am) Sait from Ankara. I got here today.
   My goodness, Sait Bey. Welcome!
   Thank you, my good friend Erdoğan. How are you? Are you in good shape? I certainly hope you're fine.
   Thanks, Sait. I'm very well. And you, how are you?
   Thank you, too. What's new, Erdoğan?
   Well, Erdoğan Bey. I've got an appointment. Good-bye. Will you please tell Ahmet Bey that I'll phone him again tomorrow?
   Sure, Sait Bey! I'll tell (him). Good-bye, sir!

7. The old woman sat weeping bitterly.
8. This is the smallest of my children's friends.
9. To hear them tell it, you're alleged to have gone there a couple of times.
10. The biggest of the cities you'll see in Turkey is Istanbul.
11. Ahmet wrote that he bought two nice rugs.
12. Is it so that you've got two big trees out behind your house?
13. Ahmet! Take this money, run fast down to the tobacconist('s store, and) quickly buy two newspapers!
14. Do you know the name of the individual who purchased the newspapers?
15. I do not believe that there is a more beautiful mountain in all the world.
16. What is this fellow's job? Is he a newsman or is he a teacher?
17. We hope that Süheylâ's sister will stay with us for two or three nights.
18. Why didn't you come, Ahmet?
19. You'll be able to get here every morning at 9:30, won't you?
20. I don't believe that you'll be able to get here every morning.

Exercise B.

1. *Ahmet, 'Kitabımı bulamıyorum,' dedi.*
2. *Ahmet kendi kitabını bulamadığını söyledi.*
3. *İnşallah, bana haftada bir yazabileceksiniz.*
4. *Niçin binaya giremediniz?*
5. *Yarın Ankaraya gidebilecek misiniz?*
6. *Girebilir miyim?*
7. *Bunu iyi okuyabileceğinizi biliyorum.*
8. *Onların niçin gelemediklerini biliyor musunuz?*
9. *Ahmedin otomobilin anahtarını bulamıyacağı bellidir.*
10. *Bütün okuduğum kitaplardan en iyisinin bu olduğunu söyliyebilirim.*

Lesson 20

Exercise A.

1. Why didn't you eat?
2. What do you say, sir? Should I go there today, or not?
3. No matter who comes, I'll give this book only to Ahmet Bey.
4. Must you really go in (after) one hour?
5. If you'll just glance (look once thus) at the watch in your hand, you'll see that it's nine thirty.
6. I am afraid that no one can come here tomorrow.
7. They weren't obliged to come here immediately.
8. Do you know why she couldn't phone?
9. It doesn't snow in our city.
10. Erdoğan's wife said that her mother had been sick for two months but had then gone back to Ankara.

11. Say what you will, I saw with my own eyes that they were ready to go.
12. If he doesn't give you back the watch he took out of your big chest, you'll have to (you'll remain in the necessity to) tell his mother the truth (about it), won't you?
13. Let her do what she wants. (Let her do it the way she wants.)
14. Hey, kids! Time's going fast. Come, let's go!
15. Sir, with your permission may I take a small bit of bread?
16. My son preferred to go to the movies rather than go to school.
17. You don't know where the bookshop Ahmet described to us yesterday is, do you?
18. They didn't say that he hadn't gone, did they?
19. They couldn't say that he wouldn't go, could they?
20. Don't you know that he can't come?

Exercise B.

1. *Size bir fincan çay vereyim mi, efendim?*
2. *Ben gitmezsem siz de gitmiyecek misiniz?*
3. *Neden bahsedelim?*
4. *Hakikaten gitmeli miydiniz?*
5. *Hakikaten gitmeli misiniz?*
6. *Siz ne dersiniz? Biz gidelim mi, gitmeyelim mi?*
7. *O gelirse kitabı ona vereceğiz.*
8. *Onlar ise gidemediler.*
9. *'Teşekkür ederim, efendim,' deyin.*
10. *Parayı bize vermek mecburiyetinde değildi.*

Lesson 21

Exercise A.

1. Was the teacup broken?
2. As I view it, that is something which really can't be known.
3. The books written by that man are hard to come by nowadays.
4. Ahmet was in Beyoğlu yesterday.
5. Was the cup broken by you?
6. The news was officially announced by the government.
7. They sat me down on a chair and wouldn't let me go.
8. I have to go, sir. In fact, I'm late. Good-bye for now.
   Good-bye, Mehmet Bey. I hope we'll get together again.
9. The big box wouldn't go through the door. Therefore it was let down from the window.
10. It can't be said that that man never came (comes) to our house. He has come a few times.

11. We talked about Ahmet for two hours. Then we reached a decision. Everything was agreed upon.
12. No matter what they say, we won't let (give permission to) you (to) go there.
13. Permit me to assist you, Sir!
14. I want two third-class tickets, please.
15. Have you forgotton what you yourself said?
16. By whom was this house built?
17. Didn't you ask them where they'd put the money?
18. Don't ask me that!
19. They washed in the sea.
20. If I have to go to Izmir Friday, I don't know what I'll do.
21. These new factories are being developed.
22. According to what is being said, he will never come back from Istanbul.
23. If you don't work, you won't be able to learn.
24. Who is teaching you Turkish?
25. Instead of the word *talebe* in old Turkish, today the word *öğrenci* is more frequently used.

Exercise B.

1. *Bu su içilmez.*
2. *Gelecek hafta Adanada buluşuruz. Anlaşıldı.*
3. *Bu tütün Türkiyeden getirilir.*
4. *Ahmet tütünü Mehmede getirtti.*
5. *Bu yoldan İzmir'e gidilmez.*
6. *Yol genişlettiriliyor.*
7. *Oğlum, çabuk giyin!*
8. *Bu haber hükümetçe bildirildi.*
9. *Dikkat ediniz! O kırılır.*
10. *Onun elyazısı okunmaz.*

Lesson 22

Exercise A.

1. You don't know whether Ahmet Bey will go to the movies with us tomorrow, do you?
2. While I was in Beyoğlu, some thief entered my house, silenced my dog, and took two good rugs and 500 liras.
3. Because they couldn't keep the children quiet, the teachers wrote letters of complaint to each of their fathers.
4. Goodness, Erdoğan Bey! How your son has grown! I can't believe my eyes.
5. Because we don't know which of your friends will be able to come, we still haven't decided which restaurant to eat in.

6. I can't exactly remember how many months it has been since Süheylâ Hanım took sick.
7. They had known for a long time that I couldn't come that day. Therefore I just somehow can't understand why they didn't remind you of it.
8. When the girl saw her father she began both to run and to weep.
9. If I have to stay more than two weeks in Istanbul, I'll not be able to meet with you in Ankara.
10. Since I wasn't sure whether your mother knew you had been in Ankara that week, I didn't show either her or your father the snapshot that I took there.
11. If they decide not to go there but to stay here, I'm sure they'll ask me for the books which I had promised would be sent to you.
12. Is it better for you to live in Istanbul than in Ankara?
13. As is known, one can't get into the library on holidays.
14. When the door was opened, the children ran to their places and sat down.
15. If they aren't made to unite, they'll not be able to do what they want to do.
16. The doctor would go to his office each day and receive his patients.
17. If you don't go, what will happen?
18. Although I've never gone there, they write me a letter every week and say that they are always expecting me.
19. Because the weather was bad we did not go swimming.
20. Have you forgotten that seeing is believing?

Exercise B.

1. *Kapıyı açarak otomobiline binip gitti.*
2. *Dünyanın küçüldüğünü unutmayınız.*
3. *Ahmedin bu kitabı okuyup okumadığını biliyor musunuz?*
4. *Çok çalışarak Türkçeyi iyi öğrendi.*
5. *Fiyatlar gittikçe yükseldi.*
6. *Giderken bana bir lira verdi.*
7. *Oraya gidip ona biraz para verirsek çok iyi olur.*
8. *Oraya gitmeyip burada kalmak istediler.*
9. *Oraya gitmemeye ve burada kalmaya karar verdiler.*
10. *Onların oraya gitmemeye ve burada kalmaya karar verdiklerini söylüyor.*

Vocabulary

açık *open*
açılmak (açılır) *to be opened*
açmak (açar) *to open (trans.)*
adam *man*
afyon *poppy, opium*
ağabeyi *elder brother*
ağaç (ağacı) *tree*
ağız (ağzi) *mouth*
ağlamak (ağlar) *to weep*
Ağustos *August*
Ahmet (Ahmedi) *man's name*
ak *white*
akmak (akar) *to run, flow*
akşam *evening*
akşam yemeği *evening meal*
alçak *low*
alfabe *alphabet*
alışmak (alışır) *to be or become accustomed to (with dat.)*
Ali *man's name*
âli *lofty, sublime*
Allah *God*
almak (alır) *to buy, get, take*
alo *hello (on the telephone)*
alt *bottom*
altı *six*
altın *gold*

altmış *sixty*
aman *oh! alas! my goodness!*
amma *but*
anahtar *key*
anlamak (anlar) *to understand*
anlaşılmak (anlaşılır) *to be understood, agreed*
anlatılmak (anlatılır) *to be explained*
anlatmak (anlatır) *to explain, recount, make understand*
anlayış *penetration; manner of understanding*
anlayışlı *perceptive*
anne *mother*
apartıman *apartment building*
ara *midst, interval*
arka *back*
Aralık *December*
aramak (arar) *to search for*
Arap (Arabı) *Arab*
arkadaş *friend*
Arnavutköy *'Albanian Village' (a suburb of Istanbul)*
aşağı *down*
at *horse*
ata *ancestor*
ayak (ayağı) *foot*

176

ayrılmak (ayrılır) *to depart, go away from*

az *few, (a) little, insufficient; less*

baba *father*

bacak (bacağı) *leg*

bahçe *garden, yard*

bahçeli *having a garden*

bahsetmek *to discuss, talk about (with abl.), to mention*

bakmak (bakar) *to look, look at (with dat.), look after (with dat.)*

bando *band (musical)*

banka *bank*

bankacı *banker*

bankacılık *the banking business*

bardak (bardağı) *drinking glass*

baş *head*

başka *another; other than (with abl.)*

başlamak (başlar) *to start to (with dat.)*

Bay *Mr.*

Bayan *Mrs.; Miss*

bayat *stale*

bayram *holiday*

bazı *some (with plural)*

beğenmek (beğenir) *like, approve, enjoy (trans.)*

beklemek (bekler) *to await, wait for (with obj. def.)*

belki *perhaps*

belli *clear, evident, plain*

bembeyaz *very white*

ben *I*

beraber *together*

beri *since (with abl.)*

beş *five*

Bey *Mr.*

beyaz *white*

Beyoğlu *downtown section of Istanbul*

bıkmak (bıkar) *to get tired of (with abl.)*

biber *pepper*

bildirilmek (bildirilir) *to be announced*

bildirmek (bildirir) *to inform, announce, cause to know*

bile *even*

bilet *ticket*

biletçi *ticket man*

bilinmek (bilinir) *to be known*

bilmek (bilir) *to know*

bin *thousand*

bina *building*

binmek (biner) *(with dat.) to get on (a horse, etc.), to get in (a car, etc.), to board (a ship)*

bir *one; a, an*

birisi *someone*

birleştirilmek (birleştirilir) *to be united*

bir şey *something*

bitirmek (bitirir) *to end (trans.)*

bitmek (biter) *to end (intrans.)*

biz *we*

boş *empty*

böyle *thus, in this fashion*

bu *this, these*

buçuk *one half (used only with other numbers)*

bulmak (bulur) *to find*

bulunmak (bulunur)   *to be found; to be*

buluşmak (buluşur)   *to meet together, to convey (intrans.)*

buluşturulmak (buluşturulur)   *to be caused to meet or get together*

bulvar   *boulevard*

bura*   *here, this place*

büro   *office*

bütün   *whole, entire, all*

büyük   *big, large, great*

büyüklük   *largeness, bigness, greatness*

büyümek (büyür)   *to grow larger*

cadde   *street, avenue*

cami   *mosque*

cep (cebi)   *pocket*

Cuma (günü)   *Friday*

Cumartesi (günü)   *Saturday*

çabuk   *fast*

çalışmak (çalışır)   *to work, work hard*

çarçabuk   *extremely swift*

çarpışmak (çarpışır)   *to collide*

çarpıştırılmak (çarpıştırılır)   *to be caused to collide*

çarpıştırmak (çarpıstırır)   *to cause to collide*

çarpmak (çarpar)   *to hit, strike against (with dat.)*

Çarşamba (günü)   *Wednesday*

çarşı   *market, bazaar*

çay   *tea*

çekmek (çeker)   *to pull* fotoğraf çekmek   *to take a photograph*

çeyrek   *quarter*

çıkış   *exit; manner of going out*

çıkmak (çıkar)   *to go out of (with abl.); to go up; to come up to (with dat.); to set forth on (with dat.)*

çıplak   *naked*

çiçek   *flower* •

çocuk (çocuğu)   *child*

çocukluk   *childhood; childishness*

çok (çoğu)   *much, many, very*

çünkü   *because*

dv^2 *also, too, for X's part, in X's turn*

dağ   *mountain*

daha   *more*

daima   *always*

dakika   *minute (time)*

defa   *time, occurrence*

değil   *not (with 'to be')*

demek (der)   *to say, speak (used only with direct quotation)* Demek, gittin.   *In other words (that is to say), you went.*

demir   *iron*

deniz   *sea, ocean*

derhal   *immediately*

ders   *lesson, class*

dış   *outside*

dışarı   *outside*

diğer   *(the) other*

dikkat   *caution* dikkat etmek   *to be careful (with dat.), to pay attention*

dilim   *slice*

diş   *tooth*

doğru   *right, true, straight; straight toward (with dat.)*

doğruluk   *rightness, straightness*

doksan *ninety*

dokuz *nine*

dolar *dollar*

dolayı *because of* (*with abl.*)

dönmek (döner) *to turn* (*intrans.*); *to return, go back to* (*with dat.*)

dört (dördü) *four*

dükkân *shop, store*

dün *yesterday*

dünya *world*

edebî *literary*

efendi *gentleman, sir*

eğer *if*

Ekim *October*

ekmek *bread, loaf of bread*

el *hand*

elektrik (elektriği) *electricity*

elektriksiz *not electrified*

elektrikli *electrified*

elli *fifty*

elma *apple*

emin *certain of, sure of* (*with abl. or dat.*)

en (*the*) *most*

endişe *anxiety* endişe etmek *to worry*

Erdoğan *man's name*

erkek *male*

erken *early*

eski *old*

eş *wife, husband*

et *meat*

etmek (eder) *to do, to make* (*auxiliary verb*)

ev *house*

ev sahibi *house owner; landlord*

evvel *before* (*with abl.*)

evet *yes*

evli *married*

evlilik *matrimony*

Eylûl *September*

eyvallah (*mild exclamation, Arabic*) *Ah, by God! So be it!*

fabrika *factory*

Fahrünnisa *woman's name*

fakat *but*

fakirlik *poverty*

fazla *more than* (*with abl.*), *too much*

fena *baa*

fikir (fikri) *idea*

fil *elephant*

filim (filmi) (*photographic*) *film; moving picture*

fincan *cup*

fiyat *price*

fotoğraf *photograph*

fotoğrafçı *photographer*

Fransız *French*

Fransızca *the French language*

frenk *Frank* (*i.e. west European*)

garaj *garage*

gâvur *heathen*

gazete *newspaper*

gazeteci *newspaperman*

gazetecilik *journalism*

gece *night*

geç *late*

geçilmek (geçilir) *to be crossed over*

geçmek (geçer) *to cross over* (*with abl., dat., and acc.*)

gelişmek (gelişir) *to flourish, to develop* (*intrans.*)

geliştirilmek (geliştirilir) *to be developed*

gelmek (gelir) *to come*

genç *young*

genişletilmek (genişletilir) *to be widened*

gerek *right, proper, necessary*

getirilmek (getirilir) *to be brought*

getirmek (getirir) *to bring, to import*

gıram (or gram) *gram*

gibi *like* (*postposition*)

gidilmek (gidilir) *to go* (*impersonal*)

gidiş *manner of going*

girilmek (girilir) *to be entered*

giriş *entrance; manner of going in*

girmek (girer) *to go into* (*with dat.*)

gitmek (gider) *to go*

giyinmek (giyinir) *to dress* (*reflexive*)

giymek (giyer) *to wear* (*clothing*)

göl *lake*

gönderilmek (gönderilir) *to be sent*

göndermek (gönderir) *to send*

göre *according to* (*with dat.*)

görmek (görür) *to see*

görücü *matchmaker*

görünmek (görünür) *to be visible, to seem*

görüşmek (görüşür) *to converse, discuss*

görüşülmek (görüşülür) *to be discussed*

görüştürmek (görüştürür) *to cause to converse*

görüştürülmek (görüştürülür) *to be made to converse with each other*

göstermek (gösterir) *to display, show* (*trans.*)

göz *eye*

gözlük *eyeglasses*

güç *difficult*

güçlük *difficulty*

gülmek (güler) *to laugh*

gümüş *silver*

gün *day*

günlük *daily*

güzel *pretty, lovely, nice, fine*

güzellik *beauty*

ha *so!*

haber *news*

hafta *week*

haftalık *weekly*

hak (hakkı) *right, truth; God* bunun hakkında *concerning this*

hakikat (hakikati) *fact, reality*

hakikaten *really*

Hakkı *man's name*

hal (hali) *circumstance, situation, condition;* (*with relative gerund*) *although*

halı *rug*

hangi *which? what?*

Hanım *Mrs.; Miss*

harem *women's section of old Turkish house*

hasta *sick*

hatırlamak (hatırlar) *to remem-ber*

hatırlatmak (hatırlatır) *to cause to remember*

hava *air; weather*

havuz *pool*

hay! hay! *(exclamation of enthusiasm)*

hayat *life*

haydi *(interjection) Well! Hey! Come on!*

hayır *no (opposite of yes)*

hazır *ready, prepared*

Haziran *June*

henüz *as yet*

hep (hepsi) *all*

her *each, every*

hırsız *thief*

hiç *none; nothing; never, ever (with positive verb)* hiç bir *not a*

hisar *fortress, castle*

hoş *fortunate; pleasing* Hoşuna gider. *It pleases him. He enjoys it.*

hükümet *government*

ırmak *river*

ısmarlamak (ısmarlar) *to commend to, order*

iç *inside*

içeri *inside*

içilmek (içilir) *to be drunk (passive of 'to drink')*

için *for*

içirilmek (içirilir) *to be caused to drink*

içirmek (içirir) *to cause to drink*

içmek (içer) *to drink*

ihtiyarlamak (ihtiyarlar) *to grow old*

iki *two*

iktisadî *economic, economical*

ile *with*

ilk *first*

inanmak (inanır) *to believe (with dat.)*

indirilmek (indirilir) *to be lowered*

indirmek (indirir) *to cause to descend; to lower*

İngilizce *the English language*

inmek (iner) *to descend from, dismount, get out of (with abl. or dat.)*

inşallah *if God will; I hope . . .*

ise *(conditional sign); however, as for*

isim(ismi) *name*

iskemle *chair*

İsmail *man's name*

ispirto *spirits, alcohol*

istasyon *station*

istemek (ister) *to want, wish, desire, need, require*

iş *matter, work, job, business* iş görmek *to do work, have a job*

işte *so, thus, all right, etc.*

İtalya *Italy*

itmek (iter) *to push*

iyi *good*

iyileşmek (iyileşir) *to grow better, improve (intrans.)*

iyilik *goodness, the good*

Japonya *Japan*

kaatil   *murderer*

kaç   *how much? how many?*

kaçışmak (kaçışır)   (*for all*) *to flee; to run off in different directions*

kaçmak (kaçar)   *to flee*

kadar   *amount; up to* (*with dat.*)

kadın   *woman*

kahvaltı   *breakfast*   kahvaltı yapmak   *to eat breakfast*

kahve   *coffee; coffeehouse*

kalem   *pencil*

kalmak (kalır)   *to stay, remain in* (*with loc.*)

kapalı   *covered; roofed-over*

kapı   *door*

kapıcı   *doorkeeper, concièrge*

kar   *snow*

kâr   *profit*

kara   *black*

Karaköy   *a section of downtown Istanbul*

karar   *decision*   karar vermek (*with dat.*) *to decide*

kardeş   *brother*

karı   *wife*

karşı   *against, opposite*

kasaba   *town*

Kasım   *November*

kat (katı)   *floor, story* (*of a building*)

katil (katli)   *murder*

kedi   *cat*

kelime   *word*

kendi   *self; own*

kere   *time, occurrence*

kılmak (kılır)   *to make, do* (*archaic*)

kırılmak (kırılır)   *to be broken; to break* (*intrans.*)

kırk   *forty*

kırmak (kırar)   *to break* (*trans.*)

kısa   *short*

kısım (kısmı)   *section, part*

kız   *girl, daughter, maiden, female*

kızkardeş   *sister*

kızıl   *red, scarlet*

kızmak (kızar)   *to become angry*

ki   *that* (*relative*)

kilo   *kilogram*

kilometre   *kilometer*

kim   *who?*

kimse   *nobody*

kira   *rent*   kirara vermek   *to rent* (*to some one*)

kiralık   *for rent*

kişi   *person*

kitap (kitabı)   *book*

kitapçı   *bookseller*

kitapçılık   *the book business*

klinik   *doctor's office, clinic*

koca   *husband*

kol   *arm*

kolay   *easy*

konuşmak (konuşur)   *to talk, converse*

korkmak (korkar)   *to be afraid of* (*with abl.*)

koşmak (koşar)   *to run*

koymak (koyar)   *to put, place* (*with dative of the place into which the object is put*)

köpek *dog*
körfez *gulf*
köy *village*
kul *slave, subject; worshiper*
kulak *ear*
kullanılmak (kullanır) *to be used*
kuruş *kuruş (piaster, 1/100 of a Turkish Lira: unit of money)*
kutu *box*
küçük *small, little*
küçülmck (küçülür) *to grow smaller*
kütüphane *library*
-l V² *(See* ile.*)*
lâle *tulip*
lamba *lamp, light bulb; radio tube*
lâzım *necessary*
limon *lemon*
limonlu *with lemon*
lira *lira (pound: unit of money)*
lisan *language, tongue*
lokanta *restaurant*
Londra *London*
lûtfen *please*
Lübnan *the Lebanon*
Lübnanî *Lebanese*
m V⁴ *(spoken question mark)*
maalesef *unfortunately*
marmara *marble*
Mart *March*
maşallah *my goodness! (Arabic: what God wills)*
Mayıs *May*
mecburiyet *necessity, obligation*

mecmua *magazine*
Mehmet (Mehmedi) *man's name (Arabic Muhammad)*
Mehmetçik *Turkey's G.I. Joe, Tommy Atkins*
mektep (mektebi) *school*
mektup (mektubu) *letter*
merhaba *hello (informal greeting)*
metre *meter*
mevcut *extant*
mevki *class, rank*
meyva *fruit*
Mihri *woman's name*
millî *national*
milyar *billion*
milyon *million*
minare *minaret*
Mösyö *Monsieur*
muallim *teacher*
muallimlik *pedagogy*
mutlaka *positively*
müsaade *permission*
namaz kılmak *to perform the formal Moslem prayer ritual*
nasıl? *how? what sort of?*
nazaran *in view of, according to (with dat.)*
nazır *overlooking, looking out upon (with dat.)*
ne? *what?*
ne (exclamatory) *how very!*
ne . . . ne (negative) *neither . . . nor. (with positive or negative verb)*
nere*? *where? what place?*
netice *result, consequence*

ne zaman? *when? what time?*

niçin (ne için)? *why?*

Nilüfer *water lily; woman's name*

Nisan *April*

not *grade, mark*

numara *grade, mark*

o *he, she, it; that, those (demonstrative)*

Ocak *January*

oda *room*

oğul (oğlu) *son*

ok *arrow*

okul *school*

okumak (okur) *to read, to study*

okunmak (okunur) *to be read*

olmak (olur) *to become, happen*

olunmak (olunur) *to be*

on *ten*

onlar *they*

ora* *there, that place*

otel *hotel*

otobüs *bus*

otomobil *automobile*

oturmak (oturur) *to sit, dwell*

oturtmak (oturur) *to cause to sit or dwell*

oturtulmak (oturtulur) *to be caused to sit or dwell*

otuz *thirty*

oynamak (oynar) *to play*

öbür *the other*

öbür gün *the day after tomorrow*

öğle *noon*

öğle yemeği *noon meal*

öğrenci *pupil*

öğrenmek (öğrenir) *to learn*

öğretmek (öğretir) *to teach*

öğretmen *teacher*

ölmek (ölür) *to die*

ön *front*

öyle *thus, in that fashion*

pahalı *expensive*

para *money*

paralı *rich*

parasız *moneyless*

parasızlık *poverty*

parça *part*

pasaport *passport*

Pazar (günü) *Sunday*

Pazartesi (günü) *Monday*

pek *very, very much*

pencere *window*

Perşembe günü *Thursday*

peynir *cheese*

pişirmek (pişirir) *to cook (trans.)*

polis *police*

portakal *orange*

postacı *mailman*

pul *stamp (postage, etc.)*

radyo *radio*

rağmen *despite (with dat.)*

randevu *appointment*

renk (rengi) *color*

resmen *officially*

rica *request*

Rus *Russian*

saat (saati) *hour, time; watch, clock*

sabah *morning*

saç *hair*

sahip (sahibi) *owner, master*

Sait (Saidi) *man's name*

sakın *in any case, at any cost, but*

Salı (günü) *Tuesday*

sanat (sanati) *art, craft*

saniye *second (time)*

satılık *for sale*

satın almak *to buy*

satmak (satar) *to sell*

sebep (sebebi) *reason, cause*

sekiz *eight*

seksen *eighty*

selâmlık *men's section of old Turkish house*

Selim *man's name*

Selma *woman's name*

sen *you (familiar singular)*

sene *year*

sevinmek (sevinir) *to be or become happy*

sevmek (sever) *to like; to love*

seyahat *travel, trip*

seyahat etmek *to travel*

sıcak *hot*

sıra *line, rank, file*

sinema *movie house*

siyah *black*

siz *you (polite singular, normal plural)*

sokak (sokağı) *street*

son *last*

sonra *after (with abl.)*

sormak (sorar) *to ask* Mehmet bana onu sordu. *Mehmet asked me (about) it.*

söylemek (söyler) *to speak, say, tell (not used with direct quotations: see* demek)

söylenmek *to be said*

söz *word; promise*

sözcü *speaker*

su *water*

Suat (Suati) *woman's or man's name*

susturmak (susturur) *to cause to be silent*

susuz *waterless*

susuzluk *aridity*

süt *milk*

sütlü *with milk*

Süheylâ *woman's name*

Şam *Damascus*

Şamî *Damascene*

şair *poet*

şehir (şehri) *city*

şeker *sugar; candy*

şekerli *with sugar*

şekersiz *without sugar*

şey *thing; uh- uh- ahem . . . (said when one hesitates in speech)*

şikâyet *complaint* şikâyet etmek *to complain*

şimdi *now*

şimdilik *for the present*

şirket *company, firm (business)*

şöyle *thus; in that fashion; as follows*

şu *that, those (demonstrative); at some distance away; which follow(s)*

Şubat *February*

Taksim *a downtown section of Istanbul*

talebe *student*

tane *counting word*

taraf *side; part; (used to express agent with passive)*

tarif etmek *to describe, define*

taş *stone*

telefon etmek *to telephone*

Temmuz *July*

tercih etmek *to prefer (with obj. def.)*

teşekkür etmek *to thank*

tiyatro *theater*

top *ball, sphere*

tramvay *streetcar*

tren *train*

tutmak (tutar) *to grasp, hold, catch*

tuz *salt*

tuzluk *saltcellar*

tuzluluk *saltiness*

tuzsuz *salt free*

tuzsuzluk *saltlessness*

Türk *Turk; Turkish*

Türkçe *the Turkish language*

Türkiye *Turkey*

türlü *fashion*

tütün *tobacco*

tütüncü *tobacconist*

ucuz *cheap, inexpensive*

uçak *airplane*

ufak *small*

unutmak (unutur) *to forget*

uzun *long, tall*

üç *three*

ümit (ümidi) *hope*

üniversite *university*

üst *top*

üzere (üzre) *over, upon, on the point of, for the purpose of*

vapur *steamer, ferry*

var *extant*

vaz geçmek *to change one's mind about (with abl.)*

ve *and*

verilmek (verilir) *to be given*

vermek (verir) *to give to (with dat. or acc.)*

ya *and as for . . .*

ya . . . ya *either . . . or*

yağ *grease, (cooking) fat; (vegetable) oil*

yağmak (yağar) *to fall as precipitation*

yağmur *rain*

yağmurlu *rainy*

yalan *lie, falsehood*

yalnız *only, alone*

yan *side*

yani *that is, i.e., I mean*

yapılmak (yapılır) *to be made*

yapmak (yapar) *to make, do*

yaramazlık *mischief*

yardım *help*

yarım *one half (not used with other numbers)*

yaş *age (of humans)*

yaşlı *old (of humans)*

yatak *bed*

yavaş *slowly*

yazı *writing, article*

yazıcı *secretary (usually in the armed forces)*

yazık   *a pity, too bad*
yazmak (yazar)   *to write*
yedi   *seven*
yemek (yer)   *to eat*
yemek   *food, meal*   yemek yemek
  to eat a meal
yeni   *new*
yer   *place, location*
yetmiş   *seventy*
yıkamak (yıkar)   *to wash (trans.)*
yıkanmak (yıkanır)   *to wash*
  (reflexive)
yıl   *year*
yılmak (yılar)   *to flinch*
yine   *again*

yok   *non-extant*
yol   *road, voyage*
yukarı   *up*
yumuşak   *soft*
yüksek   *high, tall*
yükselmek (yükselir)   *to grow higher*
yüz   *face; hundred*
yüzmek (yüzer)   *to swim*
zaman   *time*   bazı zaman   *sometimes*   bir zamanlar   *sometimes*
zaten   *as a matter of fact, in reality, at any rate*
zengin   *wealthy*
zira   *because*

A CATALOG OF SELECTED
DOVER BOOKS
IN ALL FIELDS OF INTEREST

A CATALOG OF SELECTED DOVER
BOOKS IN ALL FIELDS OF INTEREST

CONCERNING THE SPIRITUAL IN ART, Wassily Kandinsky. Pioneering work by father of abstract art. Thoughts on color theory, nature of art. Analysis of earlier masters. 12 illustrations. 80pp. of text. 5⅜ x 8½.			0-486-23411-8

CELTIC ART: The Methods of Construction, George Bain. Simple geometric techniques for making Celtic interlacements, spirals, Kells-type initials, animals, humans, etc. Over 500 illustrations. 160pp. 9 x 12. (Available in U.S. only.)			0-486-22923-8

AN ATLAS OF ANATOMY FOR ARTISTS, Fritz Schider. Most thorough reference work on art anatomy in the world. Hundreds of illustrations, including selections from works by Vesalius, Leonardo, Goya, Ingres, Michelangelo, others. 593 illustrations. 192pp. 7⅛ x 10¼.			0-486-20241-0

CELTIC HAND STROKE-BY-STROKE (Irish Half-Uncial from "The Book of Kells"): An Arthur Baker Calligraphy Manual, Arthur Baker. Complete guide to creating each letter of the alphabet in distinctive Celtic manner. Covers hand position, strokes, pens, inks, paper, more. Illustrated. 48pp. 8¼ x 11.			0-486-24336-2

EASY ORIGAMI, John Montroll. Charming collection of 32 projects (hat, cup, pelican, piano, swan, many more) specially designed for the novice origami hobbyist. Clearly illustrated easy-to-follow instructions insure that even beginning papercrafters will achieve successful results. 48pp. 8¼ x 11.			0-486-27298-2

BLOOMINGDALE'S ILLUSTRATED 1886 CATALOG: Fashions, Dry Goods and Housewares, Bloomingdale Brothers. Famed merchants' extremely rare catalog depicting about 1,700 products: clothing, housewares, firearms, dry goods, jewelry, more. Invaluable for dating, identifying vintage items. Also, copyright-free graphics for artists, designers. Co-published with Henry Ford Museum & Greenfield Village. 160pp. 8¼ x 11.			0-486-25780-0

THE ART OF WORLDLY WISDOM, Baltasar Gracian. "Think with the few and speak with the many," "Friends are a second existence," and "Be able to forget" are among this 1637 volume's 300 pithy maxims. A perfect source of mental and spiritual refreshment, it can be opened at random and appreciated either in brief or at length. 128pp. 5⅜ x 8½.			0-486-44034-6

JOHNSON'S DICTIONARY: A Modern Selection, Samuel Johnson (E. L. McAdam and George Milne, eds.). This modern version reduces the original 1755 edition's 2,300 pages of definitions and literary examples to a more manageable length, retaining the verbal pleasure and historical curiosity of the original. 480pp. 5³⁄₁₆ x 8¼.			0-486-44089-3

ADVENTURES OF HUCKLEBERRY FINN, Mark Twain, Illustrated by E. W. Kemble. A work of eternal richness and complexity, a source of ongoing critical debate, and a literary landmark, Twain's 1885 masterpiece about a barefoot boy's journey of self-discovery has enthralled readers around the world. This handsome clothbound reproduction of the first edition features all 174 of the original black-and-white illustrations. 368pp. 5⅜ x 8½.			0-486-44322-1

STICKLEY CRAFTSMAN FURNITURE CATALOGS, Gustav Stickley and L. & J. G. Stickley. Beautiful, functional furniture in two authentic catalogs from 1910. 594 illustrations, including 277 photos, show settles, rockers, armchairs, reclining chairs, bookcases, desks, tables. 183pp. 6½ x 9¼.   0-486-23838-5

AMERICAN LOCOMOTIVES IN HISTORIC PHOTOGRAPHS: 1858 to 1949, Ron Ziel (ed.). A rare collection of 126 meticulously detailed official photographs, called "builder portraits," of American locomotives that majestically chronicle the rise of steam locomotive power in America. Introduction. Detailed captions. xi+ 129pp. 9 x 12.   0-486-27393-8

AMERICA'S LIGHTHOUSES: An Illustrated History, Francis Ross Holland, Jr. Delightfully written, profusely illustrated fact-filled survey of over 200 American lighthouses since 1716. History, anecdotes, technological advances, more. 240pp. 8 x 10¾.
                                                           0-486-25576-X

TOWARDS A NEW ARCHITECTURE, Le Corbusier. Pioneering manifesto by founder of "International School." Technical and aesthetic theories, views of industry, economics, relation of form to function, "mass-production split" and much more. Profusely illustrated. 320pp. 6⅛ x 9¼. (Available in U.S. only.)   0-486-25023-7

HOW THE OTHER HALF LIVES, Jacob Riis. Famous journalistic record, exposing poverty and degradation of New York slums around 1900, by major social reformer. 100 striking and influential photographs. 233pp. 10 x 7⅞.   0-486-22012-5

FRUIT KEY AND TWIG KEY TO TREES AND SHRUBS, William M. Harlow. One of the handiest and most widely used identification aids. Fruit key covers 120 deciduous and evergreen species; twig key 160 deciduous species. Easily used. Over 300 photographs. 126pp. 5⅜ x 8½.   0-486-20511-8

COMMON BIRD SONGS, Dr. Donald J. Borror. Songs of 60 most common U.S. birds: robins, sparrows, cardinals, bluejays, finches, more—arranged in order of increasing complexity. Up to 9 variations of songs of each species.
                                       Cassette and manual 0-486-99911-4

ORCHIDS AS HOUSE PLANTS, Rebecca Tyson Northen. Grow cattleyas and many other kinds of orchids—in a window, in a case, or under artificial light. 63 illustrations. 148pp. 5⅜ x 8½.   0-486-23261-1

MONSTER MAZES, Dave Phillips. Masterful mazes at four levels of difficulty. Avoid deadly perils and evil creatures to find magical treasures. Solutions for all 32 exciting illustrated puzzles. 48pp. 8¼ x 11.   0-486-26005-4

MOZART'S DON GIOVANNI (DOVER OPERA LIBRETTO SERIES), Wolfgang Amadeus Mozart. Introduced and translated by Ellen H. Bleiler. Standard Italian libretto, with complete English translation. Convenient and thoroughly portable—an ideal companion for reading along with a recording or the performance itself. Introduction. List of characters. Plot summary. 121pp. 5¼ x 8½.   0-486-24944-1

FRANK LLOYD WRIGHT'S DANA HOUSE, Donald Hoffmann. Pictorial essay of residential masterpiece with over 160 interior and exterior photos, plans, elevations, sketches and studies. 128pp. 9¼ x 10¾.   0-486-29120-0

THE CLARINET AND CLARINET PLAYING, David Pino. Lively, comprehensive work features suggestions about technique, musicianship, and musical interpretation, as well as guidelines for teaching, making your own reeds, and preparing for public performance. Includes an intriguing look at clarinet history. "A godsend," *The Clarinet,* Journal of the International Clarinet Society. Appendixes. 7 illus. 320pp. 5⅜ x 8½. 0-486-40270-3

HOLLYWOOD GLAMOR PORTRAITS, John Kobal (ed.). 145 photos from 1926-49. Harlow, Gable, Bogart, Bacall; 94 stars in all. Full background on photographers, technical aspects. 160pp. 8⅜ x 11¼. 0-486-23352-9

THE RAVEN AND OTHER FAVORITE POEMS, Edgar Allan Poe. Over 40 of the author's most memorable poems: "The Bells," "Ulalume," "Israfel," "To Helen," "The Conqueror Worm," "Eldorado," "Annabel Lee," many more. Alphabetic lists of titles and first lines. 64pp. 5³⁄₁₆ x 8¼. 0-486-26685-0

PERSONAL MEMOIRS OF U. S. GRANT, Ulysses Simpson Grant. Intelligent, deeply moving firsthand account of Civil War campaigns, considered by many the finest military memoirs ever written. Includes letters, historic photographs, maps and more. 528pp. 6⅛ x 9¼. 0-486-28587-1

POE ILLUSTRATED: Art by Doré, Dulac, Rackham and Others, selected and edited by Jeff A. Menges. More than 100 compelling illustrations, in brilliant color and crisp black-and-white, include scenes from "The Raven," "The Pit and the Pendulum," "The Gold-Bug," and other stories and poems. 96pp. 8⅜ x 11. 0-486-45746-X

RUSSIAN STORIES/RUSSKIE RASSKAZY: A Dual-Language Book, edited by Gleb Struve. Twelve tales by such masters as Chekhov, Tolstoy, Dostoevsky, Pushkin, others. Excellent word-for-word English translations on facing pages, plus teaching and study aids, Russian/English vocabulary, biographical/critical introductions, more. 416pp. 5⅜ x 8½. 0-486-26244-8

PHILADELPHIA THEN AND NOW: 60 Sites Photographed in the Past and Present, Kenneth Finkel and Susan Oyama. Rare photographs of City Hall, Logan Square, Independence Hall, Betsy Ross House, other landmarks juxtaposed with contemporary views. Captures changing face of historic city. Introduction. Captions. 128pp. 8¼ x 11. 0-486-25790-8

NORTH AMERICAN INDIAN LIFE: Customs and Traditions of 23 Tribes, Elsie Clews Parsons (ed.). 27 fictionalized essays by noted anthropologists examine religion, customs, government, additional facets of life among the Winnebago, Crow, Zuni, Eskimo, other tribes. 480pp. 6⅛ x 9¼. 0-486-27377-6

TECHNICAL MANUAL AND DICTIONARY OF CLASSICAL BALLET, Gail Grant. Defines, explains, comments on steps, movements, poses and concepts. 15-page pictorial section. Basic book for student, viewer. 127pp. 5⅜ x 8½. 0-486-21843-0

THE MALE AND FEMALE FIGURE IN MOTION: 60 Classic Photographic Sequences, Eadweard Muybridge. 60 true-action photographs of men and women walking, running, climbing, bending, turning, etc., reproduced from a rare 19th-century masterpiece. vi + 121pp. 9 x 12. 0-486-24745-7

ANIMALS: 1,419 Copyright-Free Illustrations of Mammals, Birds, Fish, Insects, etc., Jim Harter (ed.). Clear wood engravings present, in extremely lifelike poses, over 1,000 species of animals. One of the most extensive pictorial sourcebooks of its kind. Captions. Index. 284pp. 9 x 12. 0-486-23766-4

1001 QUESTIONS ANSWERED ABOUT THE SEASHORE, N. J. Berrill and Jacquelyn Berrill. Queries answered about dolphins, sea snails, sponges, starfish, fishes, shore birds, many others. Covers appearance, breeding, growth, feeding, much more. 305pp. 5¼ x 8¼. 0-486-23366-9

ATTRACTING BIRDS TO YOUR YARD, William J. Weber. Easy-to-follow guide offers advice on how to attract the greatest diversity of birds: birdhouses, feeders, water and waterers, much more. 96pp. 5³⁄₁₆ x 8¼. 0-486-28927-3

MEDICINAL AND OTHER USES OF NORTH AMERICAN PLANTS: A Historical Survey with Special Reference to the Eastern Indian Tribes, Charlotte Erichsen-Brown. Chronological historical citations document 500 years of usage of plants, trees, shrubs native to eastern Canada, northeastern U.S. Also complete identifying information. 343 illustrations. 544pp. 6½ x 9¼. 0-486-25951-X

STORYBOOK MAZES, Dave Phillips. 23 stories and mazes on two page spreads: Wizard of Oz, Treasure Island, Robin Hood, etc. Solutions. 64pp. 8¼ x 11. 0-486-23628-5

AMERICAN NEGRO SONGS: 230 Folk Songs and Spirituals, Religious and Secular, John W. Work. This authoritative study traces the African influences of songs sung and played by black Americans at work, in church, and as entertainment. The author discusses the lyric significance of such songs as "Swing Low, Sweet Chariot," "John Henry," and others and offers the words and music for 230 songs. Bibliography. Index of Song Titles. 272pp. 6½ x 9¼. 0-486-40271-1

MOVIE-STAR PORTRAITS OF THE FORTIES, John Kobal (ed.). 163 glamor, studio photos of 106 stars of the 1940s: Rita Hayworth, Ava Gardner, Marlon Brando, Clark Gable, many more. 176pp. 8⅜ x 11¼. 0-486-23546-7

YEKL and THE IMPORTED BRIDEGROOM AND OTHER STORIES OF YIDDISH NEW YORK, Abraham Cahan. Film Hester Street based on Yekl (1896). Novel, other stories among first about Jewish immigrants on N.Y.'s East Side. 240pp. 5⅜ x 8½. 0-486-22427-9

SELECTED POEMS, Walt Whitman. Generous sampling from Leaves of Grass. Twenty-four poems include "I Hear America Singing," "Song of the Open Road," "I Sing the Body Electric," "When Lilacs Last in the Dooryard Bloom'd," "O Captain! My Captain!"—all reprinted from an authoritative edition. Lists of titles and first lines. 128pp. 5³⁄₁₆ x 8¼. 0-486-26878-0

SONGS OF EXPERIENCE: Facsimile Reproduction with 26 Plates in Full Color, William Blake. 26 full-color plates from a rare 1826 edition. Includes "The Tyger," "London," "Holy Thursday," and other poems. Printed text of poems. 48pp. 5¼ x 7. 0-486-24636-1

THE BEST TALES OF HOFFMANN, E. T. A. Hoffmann. 10 of Hoffmann's most important stories: "Nutcracker and the King of Mice," "The Golden Flowerpot," etc. 458pp. 5⅜ x 8½. 0-486-21793-0

THE BOOK OF TEA, Kakuzo Okakura. Minor classic of the Orient: entertaining, charming explanation, interpretation of traditional Japanese culture in terms of tea ceremony. 94pp. 5⅜ x 8½. 0-486-20070-1

FRENCH STORIES/CONTES FRANÇAIS: A Dual-Language Book, Wallace Fowlie. Ten stories by French masters, Voltaire to Camus: "Micromegas" by Voltaire; "The Atheist's Mass" by Balzac; "Minuet" by de Maupassant; "The Guest" by Camus, six more. Excellent English translations on facing pages. Also French-English vocabulary list, exercises, more. 352pp. 5⅜ x 8½. 0-486-26443-2

CHICAGO AT THE TURN OF THE CENTURY IN PHOTOGRAPHS: 122 Historic Views from the Collections of the Chicago Historical Society, Larry A. Viskochil. Rare large-format prints offer detailed views of City Hall, State Street, the Loop, Hull House, Union Station, many other landmarks, circa 1904-1913. Introduction. Captions. Maps. 144pp. 9⅜ x 12¼. 0-486-24656-6

OLD BROOKLYN IN EARLY PHOTOGRAPHS, 1865–1929, William Lee Younger. Luna Park, Gravesend race track, construction of Grand Army Plaza, moving of Hotel Brighton, etc. 157 previously unpublished photographs. 165pp. 8⅞ x 11¾. 0-486-23587-4

THE MYTHS OF THE NORTH AMERICAN INDIANS, Lewis Spence. Rich anthology of the myths and legends of the Algonquins, Iroquois, Pawnees and Sioux, prefaced by an extensive historical and ethnological commentary. 36 illustrations. 480pp. 5⅜ x 8½. 0-486-25967-6

AN ENCYCLOPEDIA OF BATTLES: Accounts of Over 1,560 Battles from 1479 B.C. to the Present, David Eggenberger. Essential details of every major battle in recorded history from the first battle of Megiddo in 1479 B.C. to Grenada in 1984. List of Battle Maps. New Appendix covering the years 1967–1984. Index. 99 illustrations. 544pp. 6½ x 9¼. 0-486-24913-1

SAILING ALONE AROUND THE WORLD, Captain Joshua Slocum. First man to sail around the world, alone, in small boat. One of the great feats of seamanship told in delightful manner. 67 illustrations. 294pp. 5⅜ x 8½. 0-486-20326-3

ANARCHISM AND OTHER ESSAYS, Emma Goldman. Powerful, penetrating, prophetic essays on direct action, role of minorities, prison reform, puritan hypocrisy, violence, etc. 271pp. 5⅜ x 8½. 0-486-22484-8

MYTHS OF THE HINDUS AND BUDDHISTS, Ananda K. Coomaraswamy and Sister Nivedita. Great stories of the epics; deeds of Krishna, Shiva, taken from puranas, Vedas, folk tales; etc. 32 illustrations. 400pp. 5⅜ x 8½. 0-486-21759-0

MY BONDAGE AND MY FREEDOM, Frederick Douglass. Born a slave, Douglass became outspoken force in antislavery movement. The best of Douglass' autobiographies. Graphic description of slave life. 464pp. 5⅜ x 8½. 0-486-22457-0

FOLLOWING THE EQUATOR: A Journey Around the World, Mark Twain. Fascinating humorous account of 1897 voyage to Hawaii, Australia, India, New Zealand, etc. Ironic, bemused reports on peoples, customs, climate, flora and fauna, politics, much more. 197 illustrations. 720pp. 5⅜ x 8½. 0-486-26113-1

GREAT SPEECHES BY AMERICAN WOMEN, edited by James Daley. Here are 21 legendary speeches from the country's most inspirational female voices, including Sojourner Truth, Susan B. Anthony, Eleanor Roosevelt, Hillary Rodham Clinton, Nancy Pelosi, and many others. 192pp. 5³⁄₁₆ x 8¼. 0-486-46141-6

THE MYTHS OF GREECE AND ROME, H. A. Guerber. A classic of mythology, generously illustrated, long prized for its simple, graphic, accurate retelling of the principal myths of Greece and Rome, and for its commentary on their origins and significance. With 64 illustrations by Michelangelo, Raphael, Titian, Rubens, Canova, Bernini and others. 480pp. 5⅜ x 8½. 0-486-27584-1

PSYCHOLOGY OF MUSIC, Carl E. Seashore. Classic work discusses music as a medium from psychological viewpoint. Clear treatment of physical acoustics, auditory apparatus, sound perception, development of musical skills, nature of musical feeling, host of other topics. 88 figures. 408pp. 5⅜ x 8½.　　　0-486-21851-1

LIFE IN ANCIENT EGYPT, Adolf Erman. Fullest, most thorough, detailed older account with much not in more recent books, domestic life, religion, magic, medicine, commerce, much more. Many illustrations reproduce tomb paintings, carvings, hieroglyphs, etc. 597pp. 5⅜ x 8½.　　　0-486-22632-8

SUNDIALS, Their Theory and Construction, Albert Waugh. Far and away the best, most thorough coverage of ideas, mathematics concerned, types, construction, adjusting anywhere. Simple, nontechnical treatment allows even children to build several of these dials. Over 100 illustrations. 230pp. 5⅜ x 8½.　　　0-486-22947-5

GREAT SPEECHES BY AFRICAN AMERICANS: Frederick Douglass, Sojourner Truth, Dr. Martin Luther King, Jr., Barack Obama, and Others, edited by James Daley. Tracing the struggle for freedom and civil rights across two centuries, this anthology comprises speeches by Martin Luther King, Jr., Marcus Garvey, Malcolm X, Barack Obama, and many other influential figures. 160pp. 5³⁄₁₆ x 8¼.
0-486-44761-8

OLD-TIME VIGNETTES IN FULL COLOR, Carol Belanger Grafton (ed.). Over 390 charming, often sentimental illustrations, selected from archives of Victorian graphics–pretty women posing, children playing, food, flowers, kittens and puppies, smiling cherubs, birds and butterflies, much more. All copyright-free. 48pp. 9¼ x 12¼.
0-486-27269-9

PERSPECTIVE FOR ARTISTS, Rex Vicat Cole. Depth, perspective of sky and sea, shadows, much more, not usually covered. 391 diagrams, 81 reproductions of drawings and paintings. 279pp. 5⅜ x 8½.　　　0-486-22487-2

DRAWING THE LIVING FIGURE, Joseph Sheppard. Innovative approach to artistic anatomy focuses on specifics of surface anatomy, rather than muscles and bones. Over 170 drawings of live models in front, back and side views, and in widely varying poses. Accompanying diagrams. 177 illustrations. Introduction. Index. 144pp. 8⅜ x11¼.　　　0-486-26723-7

GOTHIC AND OLD ENGLISH ALPHABETS: 100 Complete Fonts, Dan X. Solo. Add power, elegance to posters, signs, other graphics with 100 stunning copyright-free alphabets: Blackstone, Dolbey, Germania, 97 more–including many lower-case, numerals, punctuation marks. 104pp. 8⅛ x 11.　　　0-486-24695-7

THE BOOK OF WOOD CARVING, Charles Marshall Sayers. Finest book for beginners discusses fundamentals and offers 34 designs. "Absolutely first rate . . . well thought out and well executed."–E. J. Tangerman. 118pp. 7¾ x 10⅝. 0-486-23654-4

ILLUSTRATED CATALOG OF CIVIL WAR MILITARY GOODS: Union Army Weapons, Insignia, Uniform Accessories, and Other Equipment, Schuyler, Hartley, and Graham. Rare, profusely illustrated 1846 catalog includes Union Army uniform and dress regulations, arms and ammunition, coats, insignia, flags, swords, rifles, etc. 226 illustrations. 160pp. 9 x 12.　　　0-486-24939-5

WOMEN'S FASHIONS OF THE EARLY 1900s: An Unabridged Republication of "New York Fashions, 1909," National Cloak & Suit Co. Rare catalog of mail-order fashions documents women's and children's clothing styles shortly after the turn of the century. Captions offer full descriptions, prices. Invaluable resource for fashion, costume historians. Approximately 725 illustrations. 128pp. 8⅜ x 11¼.　　　0-486-27276-1

CATALOG OF DOVER BOOKS

HOW TO DO BEADWORK, Mary White. Fundamental book on craft from simple projects to five-bead chains and woven works. 106 illustrations. 142pp. 5⅜ x 8.
0-486-20697-1

THE 1912 AND 1915 GUSTAV STICKLEY FURNITURE CATALOGS, Gustav Stickley. With over 200 detailed illustrations and descriptions, these two catalogs are essential reading and reference materials and identification guides for Stickley furniture. Captions cite materials, dimensions and prices. 112pp. 6½ x 9¼. 0-486-26676-1

SIX GREAT DIALOGUES: Apology, Crito, Phaedo, Phaedrus, Symposium, The Republic, Plato, translated by Benjamin Jowett. Plato's Dialogues rank among Western civilization's most important and influential philosophical works. These 6 selections of his major works explore a broad range of enduringly relevant issues. Authoritative Jowett translations. 480pp. 5³⁄₁₆ x 8¼. 0-486-45465-7

DEMONOLATRY: An Account of the Historical Practice of Witchcraft, Nicolas Remy, edited with an Introduction and Notes by Montague Summers, translated by E. A. Ashwin. This extremely influential 1595 study was frequently cited at witchcraft trials. In addition to lurid details of satanic pacts and sexual perversity, it presents the particulars of numerous court cases. 240pp. 6½ x 9¼. 0-486-46137-8

VICTORIAN FASHIONS AND COSTUMES FROM HARPER'S BAZAAR, 1867–1898, Stella Blum (ed.). Day costumes, evening wear, sports clothes, shoes, hats, other accessories in over 1,000 detailed engravings. 320pp. 9⅜ x 12¼.
0-486-22990-4

THE LONG ISLAND RAIL ROAD IN EARLY PHOTOGRAPHS, Ron Ziel. Over 220 rare photos, informative text document origin (1844) and development of rail service on Long Island. Vintage views of early trains, locomotives, stations, passengers, crews, much more. Captions. 8⅞ x 11¾. 0-486-26301-0

VOYAGE OF THE LIBERDADE, Joshua Slocum. Great 19th-century mariner's thrilling, first-hand account of the wreck of his ship off South America, the 35-foot boat he built from the wreckage, and its remarkable voyage home. 128pp. 5⅜ x 8½.
0-486-40022-0

TEN BOOKS ON ARCHITECTURE, Vitruvius. The most important book ever written on architecture. Early Roman aesthetics, technology, classical orders, site selection, all other aspects. Morgan translation. 331pp. 5⅜ x 8½. 0-486-20645-9

THE HUMAN FIGURE IN MOTION, Eadweard Muybridge. More than 4,500 stopped-action photos, in action series, showing undraped men, women, children jumping, lying down, throwing, sitting, wrestling, carrying, etc. 390pp. 7⅞ x 10⅝.
0-486-20204-6 Clothbd.

TREES OF THE EASTERN AND CENTRAL UNITED STATES AND CANADA, William M. Harlow. Best one-volume guide to 140 trees. Full descriptions, woodlore, range, etc. Over 600 illustrations. Handy size. 288pp. 4½ x 6⅜. 0-486-20395-6

MY FIRST BOOK OF TCHAIKOVSKY: Favorite Pieces in Easy Piano Arrangements, edited by David Dutkanicz. These special arrangements of favorite Tchaikovsky themes are ideal for beginner pianists, child or adult. Contents include themes from "The Nutcracker," "March Slav," Symphonies Nos. 5 and 6, "Swan Lake," "Sleeping Beauty," and more. 48pp. 8¼ x 11. 0-486-46416-4

BIG BOOK OF MAZES AND LABYRINTHS, Walter Shepherd. 50 mazes and labyrinths in all–classical, solid, ripple, and more–in one great volume. Perfect inexpensive puzzler for clever youngsters. Full solutions. 112pp. 8⅛ x 11. 0-486-22951-3

PIANO TUNING, J. Cree Fischer. Clearest, best book for beginner, amateur. Simple repairs, raising dropped notes, tuning by easy method of flattened fifths. No previous skills needed. 4 illustrations. 201pp. 5⅜ x 8½. 0-486-23267-0

CATALOG OF DOVER BOOKS

HINTS TO SINGERS, Lillian Nordica. Selecting the right teacher, developing confidence, overcoming stage fright, and many other important skills receive thoughtful discussion in this indispensible guide, written by a world-famous diva of four decades' experience. 96pp. 5⅜ x 8½. 0-486-40094-8

THE COMPLETE NONSENSE OF EDWARD LEAR, Edward Lear. All nonsense limericks, zany alphabets, Owl and Pussycat, songs, nonsense botany, etc., illustrated by Lear. Total of 320pp. 5⅜ x 8½. (Available in U.S. only.) 0-486-20167-8

VICTORIAN PARLOUR POETRY: An Annotated Anthology, Michael R. Turner. 117 gems by Longfellow, Tennyson, Browning, many lesser-known poets. "The Village Blacksmith," "Curfew Must Not Ring Tonight," "Only a Baby Small," dozens more, often difficult to find elsewhere. Index of poets, titles, first lines. xxiii + 325pp. 5⅜ x 8¼. 0-486-27044-0

DUBLINERS, James Joyce. Fifteen stories offer vivid, tightly focused observations of the lives of Dublin's poorer classes. At least one, "The Dead," is considered a masterpiece. Reprinted complete and unabridged from standard edition. 160pp. 5³⁄₁₆ x 8¼. 0-486-26870-5

THE LITTLE RED SCHOOLHOUSE, Eric Sloane. Harkening back to a time when the three Rs stood for reading, 'riting, and religion, Sloane's sketchbook explores the history of early American schools. Includes marvelous illustrations of one-room New England schoolhouses, desks, and benches. 48pp. 8¼ x 11. 0-486-45604-8

THE BOOK OF THE SACRED MAGIC OF ABRAMELIN THE MAGE, translated by S. MacGregor Mathers. Medieval manuscript of ceremonial magic. Basic document in Aleister Crowley, Golden Dawn groups. 268pp. 5⅜ x 8½. 0-486-23211-5

THE BATTLES THAT CHANGED HISTORY, Fletcher Pratt. Eminent historian profiles 16 crucial conflicts, ancient to modern, that changed the course of civilization. 352pp. 5⅜ x 8½. 0-486-41129-X

NEW RUSSIAN-ENGLISH AND ENGLISH-RUSSIAN DICTIONARY, M. A. O'Brien. This is a remarkably handy Russian dictionary, containing a surprising amount of information, including over 70,000 entries. 366pp. 4½ x 6⅛. 0-486-20208-9

NEW YORK IN THE FORTIES, Andreas Feininger. 162 brilliant photographs by the well-known photographer, formerly with *Life* magazine. Commuters, shoppers, Times Square at night, much else from city at its peak. Captions by John von Hartz. 181pp. 9¼ x 10¾. 0-486-23585-8

INDIAN SIGN LANGUAGE, William Tomkins. Over 525 signs developed by Sioux and other tribes. Written instructions and diagrams. Also 290 pictographs. 111pp. 6⅛ x 9¼. 0-486-22029-X

ANATOMY: A Complete Guide for Artists, Joseph Sheppard. A master of figure drawing shows artists how to render human anatomy convincingly. Over 460 illustrations. 224pp. 8⅜ x 11¼. 0-486-27279-6

MEDIEVAL CALLIGRAPHY: Its History and Technique, Marc Drogin. Spirited history, comprehensive instruction manual covers 13 styles (ca. 4th century through 15th). Excellent photographs; directions for duplicating medieval techniques with modern tools. 224pp. 8⅜ x 11¼. 0-486-26142-5

DRIED FLOWERS: How to Prepare Them, Sarah Whitlock and Martha Rankin. Complete instructions on how to use silica gel, meal and borax, perlite aggregate, sand and borax, glycerine and water to create attractive permanent flower arrangements. 12 illustrations. 32pp. 5⅜ x 8½. 0-486-21802-3

EASY-TO-MAKE BIRD FEEDERS FOR WOODWORKERS, Scott D. Campbell. Detailed, simple-to-use guide for designing, constructing, caring for and using feeders. Text, illustrations for 12 classic and contemporary designs. 96pp. 5⅜ x 8½. 0-486-25847-5

THE COMPLETE BOOK OF BIRDHOUSE CONSTRUCTION FOR WOODWORKERS, Scott D. Campbell. Detailed instructions, illustrations, tables. Also data on bird habitat and instinct patterns. Bibliography. 3 tables. 63 illustrations in 15 figures. 48pp. 5¼ x 8½. 0-486-24407-5

SCOTTISH WONDER TALES FROM MYTH AND LEGEND, Donald A. Mackenzie. 16 lively tales tell of giants rumbling down mountainsides, of a magic wand that turns stone pillars into warriors, of gods and goddesses, evil hags, powerful forces and more. 240pp. 5⅜ x 8½. 0-486-29677-6

THE HISTORY OF UNDERCLOTHES, C. Willett Cunnington and Phyllis Cunnington. Fascinating, well-documented survey covering six centuries of English undergarments, enhanced with over 100 illustrations: 12th-century laced-up bodice, footed long drawers (1795), 19th-century bustles, 19th-century corsets for men, Victorian "bust improvers," much more. 272pp. 5⅝ x 8¼. 0-486-27124-2

FIRST FRENCH READER: A Beginner's Dual-Language Book, edited and translated by Stanley Appelbaum. This anthology introduces fifty legendary writers–Voltaire, Balzac, Baudelaire, Proust, more–through passages from The Red and the Black, Les Misérables, Madame Bovary, and other classics. Original French text plus English translation on facing pages. 240pp. 5⅜ x 8½. 0-486-46178-5

WILBUR AND ORVILLE: A Biography of the Wright Brothers, Fred Howard. Definitive, crisply written study tells the full story of the brothers' lives and work. A vividly written biography, unparalleled in scope and color, that also captures the spirit of an extraordinary era. 560pp. 6⅛ x 9¼. 0-486-40297-5

THE ARTS OF THE SAILOR: Knotting, Splicing and Ropework, Hervey Garrett Smith. Indispensable shipboard reference covers tools, basic knots and useful hitches; handsewing and canvas work, more. Over 100 illustrations. Delightful reading for sea lovers. 256pp. 5⅜ x 8½. 0-486-26440-8

FRANK LLOYD WRIGHT'S FALLINGWATER: The House and Its History, Second, Revised Edition, Donald Hoffmann. A total revision–both in text and illustrations–of the standard document on Fallingwater, the boldest, most personal architectural statement of Wright's mature years, updated with valuable new material from the recently opened Frank Lloyd Wright Archives. "Fascinating"–*The New York Times*. 116 illustrations. 128pp. 9¼ x 10¾. 0-486-27430-6

PHOTOGRAPHIC SKETCHBOOK OF THE CIVIL WAR, Alexander Gardner. 100 photos taken on field during the Civil War. Famous shots of Manassas Harper's Ferry, Lincoln, Richmond, slave pens, etc. 244pp. 10⅝ x 8¼. 0-486-22731-6

FIVE ACRES AND INDEPENDENCE, Maurice G. Kains. Great back-to-the-land classic explains basics of self-sufficient farming. The one book to get. 95 illustrations. 397pp. 5⅜ x 8½. 0-486-20974-1

CATALOG OF DOVER BOOKS

A MODERN HERBAL, Margaret Grieve. Much the fullest, most exact, most useful compilation of herbal material. Gigantic alphabetical encyclopedia, from aconite to zedoary, gives botanical information, medical properties, folklore, economic uses, much else. Indispensable to serious reader. 161 illustrations. 888pp. 6½ x 9¼. 2-vol. set. (Available in U.S. only.)   Vol. I: 0-486-22798-7   Vol. II: 0-486-22799-5

HIDDEN TREASURE MAZE BOOK, Dave Phillips. Solve 34 challenging mazes accompanied by heroic tales of adventure. Evil dragons, people-eating plants, bloodthirsty giants, many more dangerous adversaries lurk at every twist and turn. 34 mazes, stories, solutions. 48pp. 8¼ x 11.   0-486-24566-7

LETTERS OF W. A. MOZART, Wolfgang A. Mozart. Remarkable letters show bawdy wit, humor, imagination, musical insights, contemporary musical world; includes some letters from Leopold Mozart. 276pp. 5⅜ x 8½.   0-486-22859-2

BASIC PRINCIPLES OF CLASSICAL BALLET, Agrippina Vaganova. Great Russian theoretician, teacher explains methods for teaching classical ballet. 118 illustrations. 175pp. 5⅜ x 8½.   0-486-22036-2

THE JUMPING FROG, Mark Twain. Revenge edition. The original story of The Celebrated Jumping Frog of Calaveras County, a hapless French translation, and Twain's hilarious "retranslation" from the French. 12 illustrations. 66pp. 5⅜ x 8½.
0-486-22686-7

BEST REMEMBERED POEMS, Martin Gardner (ed.). The 126 poems in this superb collection of 19th- and 20th-century British and American verse range from Shelley's "To a Skylark" to the impassioned "Renascence" of Edna St. Vincent Millay and to Edward Lear's whimsical "The Owl and the Pussycat." 224pp. 5⅜ x 8½.
0-486-27165-X

COMPLETE SONNETS, William Shakespeare. Over 150 exquisite poems deal with love, friendship, the tyranny of time, beauty's evanescence, death and other themes in language of remarkable power, precision and beauty. Glossary of archaic terms. 80pp. 5³⁄₁₆ x 8¼.   0-486-26686-9

HISTORIC HOMES OF THE AMERICAN PRESIDENTS, Second, Revised Edition, Irvin Haas. A traveler's guide to American Presidential homes, most open to the public, depicting and describing homes occupied by every American President from George Washington to George Bush. With visiting hours, admission charges, travel routes. 175 photographs. Index. 160pp. 8¼ x 11.   0-486-26751-2

THE WIT AND HUMOR OF OSCAR WILDE, Alvin Redman (ed.). More than 1,000 ripostes, paradoxes, wisecracks: Work is the curse of the drinking classes; I can resist everything except temptation; etc. 258pp. 5⅜ x 8½.   0-486-20602-5

SHAKESPEARE LEXICON AND QUOTATION DICTIONARY, Alexander Schmidt. Full definitions, locations, shades of meaning in every word in plays and poems. More than 50,000 exact quotations. 1,485pp. 6½ x 9¼. 2-vol. set.
Vol. 1: 0-486-22726-X   Vol. 2: 0-486-22727-8

SELECTED POEMS, Emily Dickinson. Over 100 best-known, best-loved poems by one of America's foremost poets, reprinted from authoritative early editions. No comparable edition at this price. Index of first lines. 64pp. 5³⁄₁₆ x 8¼. 0-486-26466-1

THE INSIDIOUS DR. FU-MANCHU, Sax Rohmer. The first of the popular mystery series introduces a pair of English detectives to their archnemesis, the diabolical Dr. Fu-Manchu. Flavorful atmosphere, fast-paced action, and colorful characters enliven this classic of the genre. 208pp. 5³⁄₁₆ x 8¼.   0-486-29898-1

THE MALLEUS MALEFICARUM OF KRAMER AND SPRENGER, translated by Montague Summers. Full text of most important witchhunter's "bible," used by both Catholics and Protestants. 278pp. 6⅝ x 10. 0-486-22802-9

SPANISH STORIES/CUENTOS ESPAÑOLES: A Dual-Language Book, Angel Flores (ed.). Unique format offers 13 great stories in Spanish by Cervantes, Borges, others. Faithful English translations on facing pages. 352pp. 5⅜ x 8½.
0-486-25399-6

GARDEN CITY, LONG ISLAND, IN EARLY PHOTOGRAPHS, 1869–1919, Mildred H. Smith. Handsome treasury of 118 vintage pictures, accompanied by carefully researched captions, document the Garden City Hotel fire (1899), the Vanderbilt Cup Race (1908), the first airmail flight departing from the Nassau Boulevard Aerodrome (1911), and much more. 96pp. 8⅞ x 11¾. 0-486-40669-5

OLD QUEENS, N.Y., IN EARLY PHOTOGRAPHS, Vincent F. Seyfried and William Asadorian. Over 160 rare photographs of Maspeth, Jamaica, Jackson Heights, and other areas. Vintage views of DeWitt Clinton mansion, 1939 World's Fair and more. Captions. 192pp. 8⅞ x 11. 0-486-26358-4

CAPTURED BY THE INDIANS: 15 Firsthand Accounts, 1750-1870, Frederick Drimmer. Astounding true historical accounts of grisly torture, bloody conflicts, relentless pursuits, miraculous escapes and more, by people who lived to tell the tale. 384pp. 5⅜ x 8½. 0-486-24901-8

THE WORLD'S GREAT SPEECHES (Fourth Enlarged Edition), Lewis Copeland, Lawrence W. Lamm, and Stephen J. McKenna. Nearly 300 speeches provide public speakers with a wealth of updated quotes and inspiration–from Pericles' funeral oration and William Jennings Bryan's "Cross of Gold Speech" to Malcolm X's powerful words on the Black Revolution and Earl of Spenser's tribute to his sister, Diana, Princess of Wales. 944pp. 5⅜ x 8⅜. 0-486-40903-1

THE BOOK OF THE SWORD, Sir Richard F. Burton. Great Victorian scholar/adventurer's eloquent, erudite history of the "queen of weapons"–from prehistory to early Roman Empire. Evolution and development of early swords, variations (sabre, broadsword, cutlass, scimitar, etc.), much more. 336pp. 6⅛ x 9¼.
0-486-25434-8

AUTOBIOGRAPHY: The Story of My Experiments with Truth, Mohandas K. Gandhi. Boyhood, legal studies, purification, the growth of the Satyagraha (nonviolent protest) movement. Critical, inspiring work of the man responsible for the freedom of India. 480pp. 5⅜ x 8½. (Available in U.S. only.) 0-486-24593-4

CELTIC MYTHS AND LEGENDS, T. W. Rolleston. Masterful retelling of Irish and Welsh stories and tales. Cuchulain, King Arthur, Deirdre, the Grail, many more. First paperback edition. 58 full-page illustrations. 512pp. 5⅜ x 8½. 0-486-26507-2

THE PRINCIPLES OF PSYCHOLOGY, William James. Famous long course complete, unabridged. Stream of thought, time perception, memory, experimental methods; great work decades ahead of its time. 94 figures. 1,391pp. 5⅜ x 8½. 2-vol. set.
Vol. I: 0-486-20381-6   Vol. II: 0-486-20382-4

THE WORLD AS WILL AND REPRESENTATION, Arthur Schopenhauer. Definitive English translation of Schopenhauer's life work, correcting more than 1,000 errors, omissions in earlier translations. Translated by E. F. J. Payne. Total of 1,269pp. 5⅜ x 8½. 2-vol. set.   Vol. 1: 0-486-21761-2   Vol. 2: 0-486-21762-0

MAGIC AND MYSTERY IN TIBET, Madame Alexandra David-Neel. Experiences among lamas, magicians, sages, sorcerers, Bonpa wizards. A true psychic discovery. 32 illustrations. 321pp. 5⅜ x 8½. (Available in U.S. only.)   0-486-22682-4

THE EGYPTIAN BOOK OF THE DEAD, E. A. Wallis Budge. Complete reproduction of Ani's papyrus, finest ever found. Full hieroglyphic text, interlinear transliteration, word-for-word translation, smooth translation. 533pp. 6½ x 9¼.
0-486-21866-X

HISTORIC COSTUME IN PICTURES, Braun & Schneider. Over 1,450 costumed figures in clearly detailed engravings–from dawn of civilization to end of 19th century. Captions. Many folk costumes. 256pp. 8⅜ x 11¾.   0-486-23150-X

MATHEMATICS FOR THE NONMATHEMATICIAN, Morris Kline. Detailed, college-level treatment of mathematics in cultural and historical context, with numerous exercises. Recommended Reading Lists. Tables. Numerous figures. 641pp. 5⅜ x 8½.   0-486-24823-2

PROBABILISTIC METHODS IN THE THEORY OF STRUCTURES, Isaac Elishakoff. Well written introduction covers the elements of the theory of probability from two or more random variables, the reliability of such multivariable structures, the theory of random function, Monte Carlo methods of treating problems incapable of exact solution, and more. Examples. 502pp. 5⅜ x 8½.   0-486-40691-1

THE RIME OF THE ANCIENT MARINER, Gustave Doré, S. T. Coleridge. Doré's finest work; 34 plates capture moods, subtleties of poem. Flawless full-size reproductions printed on facing pages with authoritative text of poem. "Beautiful. Simply beautiful."–*Publisher's Weekly*. 77pp. 9¼ x 12.   0-486-22305-1

SCULPTURE: Principles and Practice, Louis Slobodkin. Step-by-step approach to clay, plaster, metals, stone; classical and modern. 253 drawings, photos. 255pp. 8⅛ x 11.   0-486-22960-2

THE INFLUENCE OF SEA POWER UPON HISTORY, 1660–1783, A. T. Mahan. Influential classic of naval history and tactics still used as text in war colleges. First paperback edition. 4 maps. 24 battle plans. 640pp. 5⅜ x 8½.   0-486-25509-3

THE STORY OF THE TITANIC AS TOLD BY ITS SURVIVORS, Jack Winocour (ed.). What it was really like. Panic, despair, shocking inefficiency, and a little heroism. More thrilling than any fictional account. 26 illustrations. 320pp. 5⅜ x 8½.
0-486-20610-6

ONE TWO THREE . . . INFINITY: Facts and Speculations of Science, George Gamow. Great physicist's fascinating, readable overview of contemporary science: number theory, relativity, fourth dimension, entropy, genes, atomic structure, much more. 128 illustrations. Index. 352pp. 5⅜ x 8½.   0-486-25664-2

DALÍ ON MODERN ART: The Cuckolds of Antiquated Modern Art, Salvador Dalí. Influential painter skewers modern art and its practitioners. Outrageous evaluations of Picasso, Cézanne, Turner, more. 15 renderings of paintings discussed. 44 calligraphic decorations by Dalí. 96pp. 5⅜ x 8½. (Available in U.S. only.) 0-486-29220-7

ANTIQUE PLAYING CARDS: A Pictorial History, Henry René D'Allemagne. Over 900 elaborate, decorative images from rare playing cards (14th–20th centuries): Bacchus, death, dancing dogs, hunting scenes, royal coats of arms, players cheating, much more. 96pp. 9¼ x 12¼.   0-486-29265-7

MAKING FURNITURE MASTERPIECES: 30 Projects with Measured Drawings, Franklin H. Gottshall. Step-by-step instructions, illustrations for constructing handsome, useful pieces, among them a Sheraton desk, Chippendale chair, Spanish desk, Queen Anne table and a William and Mary dressing mirror. 224pp. 8⅛ x 11¼.
0-486-29338-6

NORTH AMERICAN INDIAN DESIGNS FOR ARTISTS AND CRAFTSPEOPLE, Eva Wilson. Over 360 authentic copyright-free designs adapted from Navajo blankets, Hopi pottery, Sioux buffalo hides, more. Geometrics, symbolic figures, plant and animal motifs, etc. 128pp. 8⅜ x 11. (Not for sale in the United Kingdom.)   0-486-25341-4

THE FOSSIL BOOK: A Record of Prehistoric Life, Patricia V. Rich et al. Profusely illustrated definitive guide covers everything from single-celled organisms and dinosaurs to birds and mammals and the interplay between climate and man. Over 1,500 illustrations. 760pp. 7½ x 10⅛.   0-486-29371-8

VICTORIAN ARCHITECTURAL DETAILS: Designs for Over 700 Stairs, Mantels, Doors, Windows, Cornices, Porches, and Other Decorative Elements, A. J. Bicknell & Company. Everything from dormer windows and piazzas to balconies and gable ornaments. Also includes elevations and floor plans for handsome, private residences and commercial structures. 80pp. 9⅜ x 12¼.   0-486-44015-X

WESTERN ISLAMIC ARCHITECTURE: A Concise Introduction, John D. Hoag. Profusely illustrated critical appraisal compares and contrasts Islamic mosques and palaces–from Spain and Egypt to other areas in the Middle East. 139 illustrations. 128pp. 6 x 9.   0-486-43760-4

CHINESE ARCHITECTURE: A Pictorial History, Liang Ssu-ch'eng. More than 240 rare photographs and drawings depict temples, pagodas, tombs, bridges, and imperial palaces comprising much of China's architectural heritage. 152 halftones, 94 diagrams. 232pp. 10¾ x 9⅞.   0-486-43999-2

THE RENAISSANCE: Studies in Art and Poetry, Walter Pater. One of the most talked-about books of the 19th century, *The Renaissance* combines scholarship and philosophy in an innovative work of cultural criticism that examines the achievements of Botticelli, Leonardo, Michelangelo, and other artists. "The holy writ of beauty."–Oscar Wilde. 160pp. 5⅜ x 8½.   0-486-44025-7

A TREATISE ON PAINTING, Leonardo da Vinci. The great Renaissance artist's practical advice on drawing and painting techniques covers anatomy, perspective, composition, light and shadow, and color. A classic of art instruction, it features 48 drawings by Nicholas Poussin and Leon Battista Alberti. 192pp. 5⅜ x 8½.
0-486-44155-5

THE ESSENTIAL JEFFERSON, Thomas Jefferson, edited by John Dewey. This extraordinary primer offers a superb survey of Jeffersonian thought. It features writings on political and economic philosophy, morals and religion, intellectual freedom and progress, education, secession, slavery, and more. 176pp. 5⅜ x 8½.
0-486-46599-3

WASHINGTON IRVING'S RIP VAN WINKLE, Illustrated by Arthur Rackham. Lovely prints that established artist as a leading illustrator of the time and forever etched into the popular imagination a classic of Catskill lore. 51 full-color plates. 80pp. 8⅜ x 11.   0-486-44242-X

HENSCHE ON PAINTING, John W. Robichaux. Basic painting philosophy and methodology of a great teacher, as expounded in his famous classes and workshops on Cape Cod. 7 illustrations in color on covers. 80pp. 5⅜ x 8½.   0-486-43728-0

CATALOG OF DOVER BOOKS

LIGHT AND SHADE: A Classic Approach to Three-Dimensional Drawing, Mrs. Mary P. Merrifield. Handy reference clearly demonstrates principles of light and shade by revealing effects of common daylight, sunshine, and candle or artificial light on geometrical solids. 13 plates. 64pp. 5⅜ x 8½.
0-486-44143-1

ASTROLOGY AND ASTRONOMY: A Pictorial Archive of Signs and Symbols, Ernst and Johanna Lehner. Treasure trove of stories, lore, and myth, accompanied by more than 300 rare illustrations of planets, the Milky Way, signs of the zodiac, comets, meteors, and other astronomical phenomena. 192pp. 8⅜ x 11.
0-486-43981-X

JEWELRY MAKING: Techniques for Metal, Tim McCreight. Easy-to-follow instructions and carefully executed illustrations describe tools and techniques, use of gems and enamels, wire inlay, casting, and other topics. 72 line illustrations and diagrams. 176pp. 8¼ x 10⅞.
0-486-44043-5

MAKING BIRDHOUSES: Easy and Advanced Projects, Gladstone Califf. Easy-to-follow instructions include diagrams for everything from a one-room house for bluebirds to a forty-two-room structure for purple martins. 56 plates; 4 figures. 80pp. 8¾ x 6⅜.
0-486-44183-0

LITTLE BOOK OF LOG CABINS: How to Build and Furnish Them, William S. Wicks. Handy how-to manual, with instructions and illustrations for building cabins in the Adirondack style, fireplaces, stairways, furniture, beamed ceilings, and more. 102 line drawings. 96pp. 8¾ x 6⅜.
0-486-44259-4

THE SEASONS OF AMERICA PAST, Eric Sloane. From "sugaring time" and strawberry picking to Indian summer and fall harvest, a whole year's activities described in charming prose and enhanced with 79 of the author's own illustrations. 160pp. 8¼ x 11.
0-486-44220-9

THE METROPOLIS OF TOMORROW, Hugh Ferriss. Generous, prophetic vision of the metropolis of the future, as perceived in 1929. Powerful illustrations of towering structures, wide avenues, and rooftop parks—all features in many of today's modern cities. 59 illustrations. 144pp. 8¼ x 11.
0-486-43727-2

THE PATH TO ROME, Hilaire Belloc. This 1902 memoir abounds in lively vignettes from a vanished time, recounting a pilgrimage on foot across the Alps and Apennines in order to "see all Europe which the Christian Faith has saved." 77 of the author's original line drawings complement his sparkling prose. 272pp. 5⅜ x 8½.
0-486-44001-X

THE HISTORY OF RASSELAS: Prince of Abissinia, Samuel Johnson. Distinguished English writer attacks eighteenth-century optimism and man's unrealistic estimates of what life has to offer. 112pp. 5⅜ x 8½.
0-486-44094-X

A VOYAGE TO ARCTURUS, David Lindsay. A brilliant flight of pure fancy, where wild creatures crowd the fantastic landscape and demented torturers dominate victims with their bizarre mental powers. 272pp. 5⅜ x 8½.
0-486-44198-9

Paperbound unless otherwise indicated. Available at your book dealer, online at **www.doverpublications.com**, or by writing to Dept. GI, Dover Publications, Inc., 31 East 2nd Street, Mineola, NY 11501. For current price information or for free catalogs (please indicate field of interest), write to Dover Publications or log on to **www.doverpublications.com** and see every Dover book in print. Dover publishes more than 400 books each year on science, elementary and advanced mathematics, biology, music, art, literary history, social sciences, and other areas.